Love Him, Love His Kids

The Stepmother's Guide to Surviving
and Thriving in a Blended Family

STAN WENCK, EdD AND CONNIE J. HANSEN, MS

Aadamsmedia

Avon, Massachusetts

Published by
Adams Media, a division of F+W Media, Inc.
57 Littlefield Street, Avon, MA 02322. U.S.A.
www.adamsmedia.com

ISBN-10: 1-59869-894-X
ISBN-13: 978-1-59869-894-7

Printed in the United States of America.

J I H G F E D C B A

Library of Congress Cataloging-in-Publication Data
is available from the publisher.

This publication is designed to provide accurate and authoritative information with regard to the subject matter covered. It is sold with the understanding that the publisher is not engaged in rendering legal, accounting,
or other professional advice. If legal advice or other expert assistance is
required, the services of a competent professional person should be sought.
—From a *Declaration of Principles* jointly adopted by a
Committee of the American Bar Association and a
Committee of Publishers and Associations

Many of the designations used by manufacturers and sellers to distinguish
their product are claimed as trademarks. Where those designations appear
in this book and Adams Media was aware of a trademark claim, the designations have been printed with initial capital letters.

This book is available at quantity discounts for bulk purchases.
For information, please call 1-800-289-0963.

Contents

INTRODUCTION

ix

PART ONE: STARTING OFF ON THE RIGHT FOOT / 1

CHAPTER 1

Meeting His Kids and Building Relationships

3

CHAPTER 2

Helping Resistant, Shy, and Special Children

23

CHAPTER 3

Establishing Yourself as a New Couple

42

CHAPTER 4

What's Our Address?

62

CHAPTER 5

Custody Arrangements with His (and Maybe) Your Kids

73

PART TWO: DAY-TO-DAY LIFE / 85

CHAPTER 6

Listening and Relating to His Kids' Biological Mom
86

CHAPTER 7

Sharing Daddy with His Kids
105

CHAPTER 8

Creating Family Rituals of Your Own
113

CHAPTER 9

Disciplining Stepkids
129

CHAPTER 10

Basic Duties and Responsibilities
147

PART THREE: ACHIEVING LONG-TERM SUCCESS / 165

CHAPTER 11

Surviving Holidays, Birthdays, and Vacations
166

CHAPTER 12

Religion and Culture
178

CHAPTER 13

(Step)Money Matters

191

CHAPTER 14

When to Call 911

209

CHAPTER 15

Job Satisfaction for the Effective Stepmom

222

BIBLIOGRAPHY AND RESOURCES

230

INDEX

234

Acknowledgments

Only two names appear on this book's cover, but so many more have contributed to its completion. A special note of gratitude is extended to Kevin P. Erb for his conscientious editing and formatting. Appreciation is also extended to Dr. Diana Osborne and Nancy Shirley, MSW, for their insightful and candid manuscript critiques.

Lessons learned over the years from colleagues, clients, students, and friends provided much insight and have aided in framing our philosophy. Encouragement from this group helped us manage uncertain moments.

Perhaps most of all, we are indebted to some seventy veteran stepmoms who granted interviews and responded to our questionnaire. These moms who have been there provided an intimate knowledge available from no other source. Their views on preparing for successful stepmotherhood, what to expect, and what to do about it constitute the real core of this book. Their insights fill every page of *Love Him, Love His Kids*.

Finally, this work is dedicated to our families and friends. We thank them all for their enthusiasm, patience, and support during this book's creation.

Introduction

You already know the bad news: Census reports show that nearly 50 percent of first marriages fail. But did you know that around 67 percent of *second* marriages fail, and approximately 70 to 75 percent of subsequent marriages fail?

What is the number one cause of failure in a second or third marriage? You guessed it: The challenges of incorporating stepkids into the relationship. Not only do you face the everyday challenges of marriage and maintaining a harmonious union, you're now adding children into the mix. When you blend families, you throw a bunch of "new" people under the same roof (full- or part-time), yet you still have to juggle the rigors and responsibilities of daily life, meet everyone's needs, set new priorities, and get to work on time. It seems overwhelming—because it often is.

You may have heard horror story after horror story from stepfamilies trying to adjust to their new lives. We like to think that successful stepfamily partners are usually quieter about their situations—that's why you don't hear their stories! Yes, creating a successful stepfamily may be a daunting and difficult task, but it can happen. And it can bring you incredible rewards and happiness. Our objectives in writing this book were twofold: (1) to help you anticipate and accept your challenges, and (2) to assist you in developing a positive success story.

While writing this book, we interviewed numerous therapists, ministers, and counselors, as well as divorced, single, married, and remarried persons. Instead of just burying our noses in books, we went out and asked people who'd done it for their advice. We surveyed scores of current and former stepmoms, asking questions like:

- "What should women know about the father of their future stepchildren before marrying him?"
- "How do his prior marriages and relationships affect your life?"
- "Where should the new family live?"

We also asked about custody, visitation, discipline, money, and basic responsibility issues. We compiled their information with our own professional observations to give you a complete picture of what's ahead.

For Those Yet to Make a Commitment

For those of you who are simply in a relationship with someone who has children, or are about to be married to someone with children, take this opportunity to educate yourself about what might lay ahead.

First, be sure you and your partner are really right for each other. Although "opposites attract" is a catchy phrase, most relationship authorities suggest that *similarities*, not differences, make for enduring partnerships. Be sure you see honest and mutual disclosure of such issues as finances, health, job stability, life goals, and interests early in your relationship. Also, note his track record in previous relationships. His habits will most likely play out again, no matter how wonderful *you* might be. Most psychologists report that one's track record is one of the best predictors of future behavior.

Beyond personality traits, it's important to decide whether both of you are ready for a serious relationship. Do either of you have "unfinished emotional business"? Consider your own history and learn why your previous marriage or relationship ended. It's often difficult to determine what you could have done differently to obtain a more positive outcome from a failed relationship—what's important is that you set realistic expectations for your *next* relationship. Your expectations may be so unrealistic that your marriage and role of stepparent might be destined to fail before you begin. That's never a good start. Before you even begin considering the specifics of how to maintain a positive stepparenting household, you must identify exactly what your own personal needs are as a woman and a person. Ask yourself some very insightful and heartfelt questions like the following:

- What kind of person and father is this guy? Is he trustworthy?
- Are you willing to share your husband with "someone else"?
- Do you, as the adult, always expect to have the last word?
- How much invasion of your personal space can you tolerate?
- Are you willing to change how you approach holidays and vacations?
- Are you willing to change *where* you live?
- Can you learn to accept the children of another woman and treat them with respect?

- How do you feel about someone other than your own children's father in the role of decision maker and disciplinarian?

If the mere thought of addressing these things frightens you, you may need to reconsider the proposition of remarriage and stepparenthood. Or maybe you just need more time to contemplate some of the thought-provoking issues and resolves addressed in this book.

How to Use This Book

Most of us can identify with the topics included in this book's table of contents (page iii). You will probably easily pinpoint your concerns and the particular issues that are characteristic of your personal situation. Even if you think you only have problems in a certain area, please read the whole book anyway. You'll find plenty of practical tips, realistic considerations, new ideas, and thought-provoking questions to help you understand the big picture and thrive as a stepparent. You may also find answers to problems you hadn't anticipated. We'll tackle the most common situations you'll face:

- Recognizing and supporting the varied and special needs children have
- The often touchy issues of religious preferences and custody arrangements
- Dealing with and cooperating with the mother of his children
- Learning how to share your new husband with his children without resentment
- Developing your own rituals for holidays and vacations as a new family

- Assigning chores—to everyone
- Establishing yourself as a parent in the household
- Knowing when to get professional help
- Disclosing all financial obligations

In short—we'll talk about the sticky situations no one else wants to talk about!

The Joy That Awaits You

Yes, stepparenting can be challenging. But it can also be immensely rewarding—your hard work really is worth it. So much joy can come from hearing your husband's child say, "Thank you for being my mom!" Many loving, life-long bonds are created this way. Being a stepmom can be the most rewarding, satisfying, and productive role you have ever played.

Why Us?

We're uniquely qualified to write a book about stepparenting—we've both "been there, done that." Here's a little bit about our backgrounds.

Dr. Stan Wenck

After growing up in Iowa with parents who were married until they passed away, I became a father, divorce survivor, and stepdad to three strapping teenage stepsons. Did the boys and I have issues? Emphatically yes! Plus, I had a front-row seat to the ongoing relationship dilemmas between my two teenage daughters and their stepmom.

Personal details aside, I'm also a clinical psychologist and was a university professor. I've heard hundreds of accounts of relationship disputes and disasters involving stepmoms, stepdads, and stepkids, which all too often ended in divorce. I now believe that most of the misunderstandings, clashes, and festering resentments that destroy marriages are *avoidable*. If wise choices and adjustments are made *early on*, many unions with problems and challenges might still work. Almost anything's fixable unless it's too far gone. Tragically, we then throw it away and "open up" another marriage. I knew I could help others in the same situations that I encountered in my personal and professional life, and I knew stepmoms who would be willing to share their successes, failures, and ideas. This book was born.

Before we wrote this book, Connie and I developed a fifteen-question Stepmom Survey that highlighted the stepparenting issues we deemed most crucial. More than sixty stepmoms and former stepmoms revealed what their fellow stepmoms should know prior to marriage (or making a major commitment). They shared their personal experiences, struggles, coping strategies, and successes in relating to their stepchildren. Some responses were what we expected. Others were totally unanticipated, surprising, insightful, creative, and humorous. This material, from people like you and me, became the core of *Love Him, Love His Kids*.

Connie and I also did our research, of course, so the book has everything you need to establish a successful stepparenting relationship. We hope that this book will give you both preventive and healing strategies in forming healthy and happy relationships between you and your current or future stepchildren. We would appreciate any comments, suggestions, and/or experiences regarding any part of this book. Please visit the "Contact Us" link at *www.hansenandwenck .com*. E-mails will be kept in confidence.

Introduction

Connie J. Hansen

I have served as a teacher and educator in Indiana for more than thirty years. Over the years, I've also conducted workshops involving interpersonal communications, family, child relationships, staff development, and more.

I never intended to become an educator. My undergraduate background is in theatre and communications (two great assets when dealing with stepparenting!). I loved every minute of my time with both. As I did graduate work toward a degree in education, I found I could put the two together. I became a certified Reading Specialist in my school corporation and also provided direct services for children in need. Much of my time was spent with high-risk children who had both academic and emotional needs. With the divorce rate so high, many of my students came from one-parent or stepparent homes. Serving on our Crisis Intervention Team, I saw firsthand the challenges of making blended families work successfully. I also experienced those challenges in my personal life, as I became a stepmom. I used that knowledge and experience in writing this book, along with the invaluable input from stepmoms who talked with us and completed our survey. Many of the responses we received were poignant and sincere, and many were filled with the results of frustrating and unsuccessful efforts at making a seemingly impossible situation . . . possible.

It is our hope that you find this book filled with understanding, compassion, and great strategies for making your relationships happy. We hope it also provides you with a smile or two as well. You are not alone. In the jungle of stepparenting there are many of us who have made our way along the same paths, and I'm sure you will think we are speaking directly to you. Enjoy. And remember: It *is* possible!

Part One

Starting Off on the Right Foot

Chapter 1

Meeting His Kids and Building Relationships

"Tomorrow is the big day—I'm meeting his kids for the first time. I wonder what they're like. I want them to like me because I can be a really positive force in their lives. Mostly what they'll need from me is a little guidance, love, and attention. I wonder how they get along with each other? I know they will be loving and appreciative just like their father. I can teach them so many things. I just want to be a good model for them."

Would the words, "well-meaning," "realistic," or "naive" best describe these initial thoughts? Do any of these thoughts sound familiar?

Have an Open Mind

Veteran stepmoms would probably laugh out loud at that quote (from hindsight, of course). They know that it's important not to make unrealistic assumptions up front—you can't assume the kids will or won't act a certain way when you meet them. And, of course, you'll need to be patient and approach the situation with an open mind.

Before you meet your future stepchildren, try to stand in their shoes. To understand others, we need to look at things through their eyes. These kids may be a little anxious, scared, and angry. They may be blaming you for "stealing" their daddy, or being the primary reason their lives were disrupted. (Pages 12–13 teach the technique of active listening and nurturing your new stepkids' unique abilities, interests, and needs; we'll talk more about this subject then.)

If you take the time to understand where they're coming from, you'll be much more able to provide the answers and support they need when they need it. These are the first steps of building trust and becoming a confidant and positive role model.

When Should I Meet Them?

If you are at the point where you are about to meet his children for the first time, you're probably several months into your relationship. If logistics allow, wait until you both have made some type of commitment before meeting his children. Why? Younger kids, especially, could become attached and then disappointed if the relationship, for whatever reason, does not continue. Let's look at two main factors that should help determine when you meet his kids: their age and how many there are.

How Old Are the Kids?

Their age, of course, and with which parent they will live are pivotal in how you approach the situation and what your expectations should be on this first encounter:

- **Younger children may be a little easier to approach.**
  And again, attachments and bonding happen much more
  quickly.
- **Teenagers and older children,** depending upon their
  maturity level and impressions of the relationship, may be
  more hesitant before beginning to trust a newcomer like
  you. If they're used to having Dad exclusively and like
  things the way they are, gaining their acceptance will
  very likely be more challenging.
- **Adult children,** as well, may be quite reserved before
  granting their approval. Obviously, adult children might
  be less involved in your daily lives, but they will be just as
  concerned about their dad's happiness and your intentions.
  (One of our former stepmoms reported fearing actual physical danger from a stepson-in-law who viewed her as a new
  competitor for his father-in-law's fortune, on which he had
  feasted for years. The situation is rare, but it happens.)

In this chapter, we will focus primarily on children still "in the
nest," since they will have the biggest impact on your relationship.

How Many Are There?

As you can imagine, three new stepchildren make for a
more complex situation than just one. Each child is different;
each has his own loyalties. But they also have a personality as
a group and need to be "won over" as a group.

And they know that there is strength in numbers. They
may try to "toy" with you to test your character, resolve,
and strength of will. (That may sound like something out of
a movie, but it does happen to some degree.) Developing a
relationship with a group is not impossible—it simply takes
more time. It's better to wait as long as you can before meeting a group of his kids.

Preparing to Meet Them

You and your partner have probably spent many hours discussing the children involved on both sides. That's great—you want to find out what you can about their needs, characteristics, likes, and dislikes. Be careful, however, to allow yourself the freedom to explore their personalities from your own perspective as well. After all, few biological parents are totally objective about their children! Knowing this, you might also ask his friends (or other people you know who've met his kids) about them.

Though you want to get some background on the kids, don't overthink the situation. If you obsessively plan out your first meeting, you'll spend it debating with yourself if the kids are how you thought they'd be, instead of letting yourself enjoy the time with them.

Understand What They've Gone Through

A key part of starting off on the right foot is to be compassionate and understanding about what children of divorce confront. There are countless books and periodicals on the subject. Read as much as you can about the psychology of separation and broken families. The more you know, the better you can respond to their needs and anticipate their reactions.

How parents dealt with the separation will greatly affect how the children cope and learn to survive postdivorce. If the marriage was filled with anger or abuse, they may be enjoying the relative calm of the divorce. However, they are likely still wounded by the experience.

Also, remember that most children, especially young ones, never stop hoping that Mom and Dad will get back together. They may even feel disloyal to their mom if they allow themselves to like you. Young children may also feel the opposite and instead be desperate to form a new family. Keep these things in mind when you first meet the kids. Don't expect them to be overjoyed to meet you or to fall in love with you during the first meeting.

Teenagers: A Special Challenge

Teenagers can be in a class by themselves (great revelation, we know). They can be both the neediest and the most delightful. If you face some initial rejection, or the first meeting doesn't go as well as you hoped, do not give up. We repeat: Tread slowly and keep your initial expectations to a minimum.

How It Might Go

Here's a story that's pretty typical of a first meeting. Linda told us that she was so nervous about meeting her fiancé's children that she planned it for weeks. She planned what to wear, what to say, and even how to greet them. She ordered two kinds of pizza, bought soda and small gifts, and went in with high hopes. Here's what happened: the kids barely spoke, didn't like the kind of pizza or soda she bought, and barely looked at the gifts. Responses were no more than a "grunt." After fifteen minutes, the kids left to play with their friends.

Ouch! The lesson: even pizza and small gifts make for overkill during the first meeting. We're happy to report that subsequent encounters improved, but Linda felt she never got past that first meeting, which she interpreted as rejection.

Recipe for Success

Since you've learned not to expect a Hallmark moment the first time you meet them, a "successful" first meeting is simply one where you exchange a few words and smiles.

Here are some other things to keep in mind:

- Keep your initial expectations limited
- Plan a short meeting—you don't want an all-day affair
- Be genuine and sincere without trying too hard
- Be careful not to blame your future husband if the meeting doesn't go the way you had hoped.

We know this may seem extremely difficult. Be patient. You can do it. As you move forward in the relationship with your beloved and his children, getting to know each child as an individual will be a rewarding discovery. Just don't expect that discovery the day you meet them.

Got Grandsteps?

Yes, grandstepchildren, maybe even great-grandstepchildren. Grandstepparenting happens all the time. Although these little folks may be another step or two removed from you in terms of generation, they will still figure into your new blended family configuration. Depending on the custodial situation, your new partner may have even been your future grandstepkids' primary caregiver.

Of course, it works both ways. You yourself may have grandchildren. Most of the same issues regarding first-generation stepchildren apply here as well. It means having groups of step-relatives for both of you—and another degree of complexity—but also extra potential blessings! Having grandsteps may mean extra time, funds, and energy expected from you and your new mate. One stepmom mentioned, "I just love having a house full of people on holidays." That's a positive way of looking at the situation!

Your Partner's Relationship with His Kids

Right about now, you may be feeling a bit outnumbered (especially if you don't have children yourself). Your future husband may be surrounded by his children and (perhaps) his grandchildren; then there's you. If you feel that way, you're probably so intent on harmony and making it all work that you are losing sight of yourself in the mix. That's easy to do, as you are the adult and the responsibility for so much falls on you.

Watching how your partner relates to his children will give you clues as to their personalities and how you can get to know them. Not only will you learn more about his kids, but you'll also get a sense of how he will probably relate to your children if you have any. Watch for interpersonal signs and relationship cues. You can fairly easily spot if the kids are:

- Competitive
- Argumentative
- Jealous
- Possessive
- Loving
- Respectful
- Acceptant
- Reluctant

Always keep in mind that bringing someone new into a family unit can be threatening to even the most secure children. If you have children as well, another variable is added to the new unit. Knowing the kids' personality traits will help you assess what to do next. If the child is possessive of his father, don't barge in and hang all over him. If the child is reluctant, assume it will take a while before she's comfortable with you.

Setting Your Expectations of Your Stepkids

We've already mentioned several times that you shouldn't expect to be best friends with his kids from the second you meet them. What else should you know?

- **Expect them to act their age.** Do not expect his children, regardless of their ages, to be on the same maturity level as you. You are the adult, and it's your responsibility to be sensitive to their needs.
- **Have a thick skin.** Children display behaviors that are frequently indicative of deeper feelings and needs. For example, rudeness—"I hate that kind of pizza!"—might just be a sign that they're unsure of you (and your new kind of pizza!). Or their angry remarks may reveal that they are generally "mad at the world" for what they think has been unfair in the past. These remarks may actually have nothing to do with you. Knowing which is which is the real skill. (If you encounter situations like this, don't glare at your partner with a look that says, "How could you raise such thoughtless children?" Your reactions in such situations will play a huge role in how your new family comes together.)
- **Don't live in fantasyland.** If you waltz into the future intending that your children will become the Brady Bunch, be prepared for disappointment. Have lots of tissues for a backup.
- **Don't promise the moon.** Making grandiose promises ("We're all going to be one big happy family!") to his children can be a disaster.
- **Let them know what to expect from you up front.** Point out what you will and will not do such as not cleaning their rooms.

These steps increase the chances that your relationship with them will expand into something stronger and deeper.

Their Expectations of You

Just as you have certain expectations (or fantasies) about how your first meeting might go, so do his kids. We get so caught up in our own plans, needs, and anticipations that we may not stop to wonder what these children might be thinking and needing. If you and your partner are communicating well, you have discussed with him exactly what he has told them about you and how he has prepared them for this meeting.

The new stepkids-to-be probably have been and are experiencing quite a number of questions and emotions, such as:

- Is this my new mom?
- Is she cool or will she be strict?
- Will she love us as much as her own kids? (or even) Will she love us at all?
- What kind of rules will she have?
- Will she take all of Dad's time?
- Will Dad love her more than us?
- Will she interfere in our lives and change everything?
- Do we have to call her "Mom"?
- Is she a good cook?

Remember: Children are faced with so many issues when their biological parents separate. Keep in mind that these are children and you are the adult. Tell them that no question is stupid and that you're happy to meet them and look forward to getting to know them. Be sincere and genuine, because they will know if you are not. Don't barge in with hugs and forced enthusiasm. Things take time to evolve—building trust is the first step. Above all, respect their space, their privacy, and consider their needs at this time before your own.

Practice Active Listening

Did you know that people are able to understand spoken words at a rate approximately three times faster than people talk? This ability has led to the development of "compressed speech," which advertisers use to get a lot said in a very short time. What's this got to do with being a stepmom, you say? Quite a lot.

Many folks reason that, since they can listen faster than a person can talk, they can "psychologically leave" at any time and think about something else, because they can always catch up to what the speaker is saying. The problem is it doesn't work, because we miss crucial elements of what is said. And you don't want to miss anything your future stepkid says.

But you can use your speedy understanding *to your advantage*. Use the capacity of listening faster than your stepchildren talk by becoming an "active listener." That means:

1. Noting the *feeling* and *emotion* as well as the *content*
2. Mentally summarizing (to yourself) what they are saying at intervals throughout the conversation
3. Mirroring back to the speaker your summaries of his/her statement and emotion by a reflection like, "So Sally is your best friend and it kind of hurt when she didn't invite you."

This is listening at its best. It validates her feelings as being appropriate and lets her know you understand at the same time. We all cherish being understood. You demonstrate your understanding genuinely by *active listening*.

Like anything else, this kind of listening is a skill. Practice it with your friends, even with your husband—it brings people closer. And it makes people—even your future stepkids—*want* to talk with you. They appreciate someone taking the effort to really understand them.

Nurture Unique Interests and Needs

Think back to when you were a child and how important recognition was to you. Remember jumping off the diving board and yelling, "Mom! Mom! Watch!"? All people crave recognition and affirmation, but children in particular need it in order to develop self-esteem and security. Self-esteem is a huge cornerstone in developing into a productive and self-sufficient adult.

So should you foster, encourage, and reinforce the development of each stepchild's unique abilities? Yes! Whether the child's gift is in music, art, sports, or in a particular academic area, nurture it. It is your responsibility as a stepparent and caregiver. Most all of us owe our gratitude to a special person who encouraged our interest and then cheered our development in a particular area. Be that person to your stepchildren! Their enthusiasm as they deepen their learning is contagious. While they may not verbally thank you each and every time, their new learning will be fun to watch.

Accept All Kinds of Interests

Taking an interest in the things that are important to your children and stepchildren is a powerful way to help them develop a positive relationship with you. Of course, that's much easier to do if your new children like the same things you do. If you're a basketball fan, and your new stepson is a starter on his team, you just have received an added bonus in your life! Think how fun it is to immerse yourself in a sport when your family member enjoys it as much as you do.

Or, maybe you're a "girly girl" and have a stepdaughter who adores frogs, Freddy Kruger, and scary movies. While you may feel a world away from her, you still need to make an effort. Even if you don't share a child's interests, you can still respect their differences and facilitate their explorations.

Find the Time

We are all so unbelievably busy, and we race through the day trying to keep up with work, household responsibilities, homework, laundry, meals, and myriad daily demands—so extracurricular activities are easy to shove to the back burner. But keep in mind that they are incredibly important to the child. And yes, it's OK to attend soccer games, school plays, and track meets and silently count the minutes until it's over and you can go home. (We've all done that!) Those of you who take the time to coach or assist your child's, or your stepchild's, activity deserve a special place in heaven.

A note: We know you feel overworked. Someone is clamoring for dinner, while another needs help with his or her homework. In the midst of all of this, somewhere, there is *you*. Finding time for yourself is probably getting harder and harder if the kids are involved in a lot of activities, but it's so important that you find the time whenever you can to show an interest in what they're doing.

Create a Schedule

Carolyn L. shared a trick we think is very effective. She married a man with three children and brought her own two to the family. With the older three being teenagers, everyone's schedule was jammed, and both Carolyn and her new husband worked full-time. To keep everything straight, they kept a huge calendar/message board in the laundry room. Everyone posted his or her schedule and extracurricular activities. The parents initialed which of those they could attend, attempting as best as they could to make everything equitable. They also blocked out time for the family once a week, and no one was allowed to schedule anything during that time.

Was it difficult? We're talking about *five* kids here, so of course it was. But eventually they fell into a routine that they could all accept and support one another in doing. It never became so rigid that special situations were not taken into account, but it gave them a basis from which to work and accommodate the needs and interests of each child.

If You Can't Make It

If you can't attend a child's activities regularly, make other efforts to stay involved. Try these ideas:

- Say, "I'm so proud of you." It shows the child that you're paying attention and know how hard the child is working.
- Say, "Thanks for asking me to come to your soccer game." Then briefly explain why you can't make it and how you'll try to attend another game later in the season.
- Offer sincere, positive comments when you do attend and interact—they will help make up for the times when you can't.
- Take an interest and converse about their activities—it's often just as powerful as being in attendance every time they run the quarter-mile. Ask how the activity's outcome affects what happens next for the team or group.
- Remember when they have special events coming up, and ask about them after the fact if you can't make it.

Kids crave support and recognition. Be sincere, don't overpraise (they know if it's phony), stay involved as best as you can, and *listen*!

Think Outside the Box

Here are some other ideas for how to nurture a child's interests:

- Planning at-home activities is equally important. Games, family activities, TV, and backyard recreation and interaction are also important relationship builders.
- Be on the lookout for special opportunities in your child's area of interest, like museum exhibits, shows, and author signings.
- Ask yourself if someone else in your life can help you nurture a child's interests, for example, a friend, coworker, parent. When the time is appropriate, you can involve others in your quest to help your stepkids enjoy life.
- Factor in the child's emotional needs, too. Some kids need drawing out. Maybe they have fallen through the cracks in one way or another. Wouldn't it be great to help enhance their self-esteem? Active listening can be very effective here. Other children might benefit from becoming more sensitive to others' feelings. Nudge them into helping someone in need and then reinforce these behaviors. That's how to positively shape character and behavior one step at a time.

Grandparents and Stepgrandparents

Grandparents play an amazing role in the lives of their grandchildren. Those of you who are grandparents yourselves know that you have a fierce and compelling bond with these children. With more and more grandparents playing an intricate part or actually raising their grandchildren, you must take care not to underestimate their impact and involvement. Yes, some grandparents can be judgmental and interfering, but thankfully most just want to be helpful and supportive. It's difficult for parents to watch the marriages of their children fail and see what happens to children of divorce. Sometimes, grandparents' homes can provide a comfortable and safe haven for the children that remains constant and unchanging, unlike the rest of their lives. Try not to feel threatened by these generally well-intentioned people. Don't naturally assume they loved his first wife more and view you as an intruder. When you demonstrate that you genuinely care for your stepchildren and are doing your best to make the transition into a new family as cohesive as possible, you might find great advocates in your new in-laws.

Become a Positive Role Model

Cassandra Mack, CEO of Strategies for Empowered Living Inc., host of a talk show, and author of six books, asks the question, "Has it ever occurred to you that you may be the only positive influence on someone else's life?" She goes on to say that, "we may not be self-aware of it, and those who mimic us may never tell us or admit it, but the influence, particularly if positive, is there." Becoming a positive model is not always easy—you may even be at odds at times with others as a result—but it's a crucial role you must play.

We know that parents are typically the first and most significant models for children. Kids encounter them first. Parents are bigger and more powerful. And parents have frequent and intense contact with their kids, of course. Children see their parents as their protectors, their home base, and their "rock"— even when parenting is poor. It's like how baby chicks attach themselves to the first animal they see after hatching. This process, called *imprinting*, is an instinctual desire to acquire learning in this period of an animal's life. Likewise, our children attach themselves to us. They walk like us, talk like us, think like us, and usually behave like us.

Because of the crucial importance of the modeling phenomenon, we've created these seven steps in becoming a Super Model. These represent our own views, as well as the input from our stepmoms and fellow professionals:

1. **Be aware of the awesome power you have.** Set yourself on a path of self-improvement. Honestly appraise your own pros and cons. Seek feedback from others. Start with issues easiest to change. Use proven methods to improve your self-esteem. Become well rounded.

2. **Demonstrate honesty, confidence, making good choices, and being "real."** This is how to gain respect. Kids will know, one way or the other.

3. **Develop your own short-term, intermediate, and long-range goals.** Help each child develop his or hers as well.

4. **Strive to understand each child.** They will realize and appreciate this. They're not just little adults, you know.

5. **Aid them in developing and maintaining wholesome and supportive friendships.** Model the joys of giving and receiving.

6. **Help them learn from both success and failure.** Each has much to teach. Show them how to become good winners and losers.

7. **Encourage laughter, fun, and appreciation of beauty.** All have healing benefits. Foster a healthy balance between work and play.

We'll talk more about the power of positive modeling in Chapter 15.

Become a Confidante

Dictionaries pretty universally define "confidante" as a person to whom secrets are confided or with whom private matters and problems are discussed. A confidante can also be a consultant or life coach (a person who helps those seeking both personal and career advice). Stepmoms have an ideal opportunity to become invaluable confidantes (though at your first meeting, this may feel like a long way off). This comes about after cultivating the trust of stepchildren by being positive role models and keeping issues shared with them in confidence.

Stepmoms in our survey reported that stepchildren shared information and sought advice from them about issues that they were reluctant to share with either biological parent. As such, you can become quite involved in shaping kids' thinking and values. This can be both potentially very rewarding and an awesome responsibility. You'll need to use your skills of active listening and reflection to gather the information, then confront the child with any errors in their thinking that you've noticed.

The same ethics adopted by professional counselors apply also to stepparents. Keep all conversations in total confidence—except if the child tells you he wants to inflict harm on himself or others. In that case, tell the biological parents immediately. If they're not available, tell appropriate civic officials or a doctor.

Experiencing Cross-Cultural Issues? Of Course!

Maybe your new husband is from somewhere overseas. He may be of a different ethnic background. He and his kids may not embrace the same religion, politics, and ideologies as you. Or he may be from the next town, share the same religion, and speak with the same accent. Regardless of the similarities and differences existing between you and your spouse, cultural diversity is always involved. The mere fact that you and he and his kids were reared in different homes makes for a cultural difference! Ironically, the more subtle differences are often more difficult to deal with because we assume we are more alike than we really are. On the other hand, if we come from different countries, ethnicities, religions, races, credos, or codes, we know up front that our task is to learn to understand, appreciate, and benefit from these diversities.

Like appreciating differences in art, becoming acquainted with new values, foods, customs, architecture, dress, and a pace of life can be fascinating and broadening. One culture is not necessarily better than any other, it's just different. Be open to new learning, change, and adaptation. Know that you can learn from *anyone*. Your new spouse *and his children* have much of value to teach you. We'll talk about this subject again in Chapter 12.

A Case in Point: Planning Ahead

Stepmom Jean told us about planning her first meeting with her boyfriend's children. She wanted them all to have dinner at a relaxed restaurant and planned nice gifts for each of his two children. Fortunately, her friend and veteran stepmom, Cassie, gave her some good advice and two things to consider:

1. **Dinner is pretty confining** (it can be difficult to talk to people at the other end of the table) and can last longer than you might want, especially if things aren't going the way you had hoped.
2. **Buying gifts for children you don't know can set the stage for some pretty big expectations.** Older children will see right through your "trying too hard" efforts. Younger children can easily be confused by gifts and have unrealistic expectations about their relationship with you in the future (they may think you'll *always* bring gifts).

She advised Jean to set up a casual and fairly brief first meeting instead. Cassie also suggested that she not ply them with anything other than her sincere effort to be friendly and interested in them. Jean needed to be polite, but not overly so, and certainly not overdo her enthusiasm and attentions.

Jean changed her plans to a first encounter of stopping by their house and visiting briefly with her boyfriend and his kids at poolside. It was friendly, short, and without any expectations other than to meet and say hello. It went well, and it also gave her boyfriend some time afterward to process the meeting with his kids privately and get their reactions.

REFLECTIONS: KEY ISSUES IN CHAPTER 1

- Young, teen, and adult stepchildren each are uniquely challenging and uniquely rewarding.

- Don't overprepare before meeting them.

- Understand how separation and divorce might have affected them.

- Be patient. Don't expect too much too soon.

- Grandstepchildren add complexity and blessings too.

- Practice the power of active listening.

- Nurture and encourage special interests and talents.

- You can learn many strategies to become a positive role model and confidante.

- Appreciate, learn, and benefit from cultural differences.

Chapter 2

Helping Resistant, Shy, and Special Children

"Why do they stonewall me when I'm trying so hard to please them?" stepmom Christine asked. The fact is, this stonewalling may actually have little to do with Christine personally. Kids become who they are due to an interaction of genetics and their accumulation of experiences. They are what they are at this point due to their history and heredity. The key is to understand where they're coming from. Drawing out shy and resistant children takes a bit of skill and time.

Discern What Has Made the Child Angry or Shy

The months or years leading up to a divorce can result in a very chaotic, traumatic, or even abusive environment in the home. As hard as adults may try to shield their children, or as blind as they may be to what affects them, children are observant and perceptive. There is no such thing as a "painless divorce" where children are involved. Obviously, the less open the hostility or conflict, the less damaging the divorce may be to the children.

How the parents treat each other postdivorce is critical to a chance for normalcy and household peace for the children in the future. (We address these facets of behavior throughout this book.) As hard as it may be for adults to control their anger and behavior, if they love their children more than themselves, they will do it. The key is to know what situation your particular stepchildren are in so that you can help them adjust and move on.

Learn about Their Past

Even though his previous marriage is part of his past, the present walks upon its heels, and you should avail yourself of as much information as you can regarding the particulars of the marriage, divorce, and manner in which the children were raised and treated. Asking for this background has nothing to do with invading his privacy and everything to do with trying to understand what makes the children tick and who they are. Investigating their school connections, their friends, family, and past experiences can help tremendously in trying to determine what makes a child shy, hesitant, recalcitrant, hostile, or filled with anger. There may be deep and painful events in the child's life that are totally unrelated to his or her domestic situation. Find out as much as you can through positive communication and interaction with your new husband, and be ever observant with your stepchildren. You will fill a critical role in their development and emotional health.

Do not make this situation about you, and try not to take their reactions personally. Yes, you are important, but keep reminding yourself that you are the adult, and you need to help reluctant children learn to trust again—or in some cases, for the first time.

Take a Step Back

Understanding the reasons for the children's behavior is the first step in reaching out to them. Then, simply back off. Why? Because you need to give the children space and time to process and get to know you. You don't want to present the hovering and controlling stepmom image.

Janna D. told us that she couldn't understand why her stepchildren seemed to resent and hate her from the beginning; she had tried to be so nice to them. She knew their birth mom left their father for someone else. She thought they would embrace her and love the fact that they had a new mom to care for them. The reality, unfortunately, was quite the opposite. The children were filled with anger. No doubt the kids were displacing on to her the anger they felt at having to restructure their lives. After receiving good counsel from a successful stepmom and doing some reading, Janna's understanding improved markedly. She began to accept his kids' anger, and they, in turn, began to accept her. It's all about knowing where they're coming from.

How can you measure what abandonment feels like to children? You can't, so don't guess or assume you know. The road to trusting can be a long and hard one, but one the kids need to travel.

Build a Relationship by Backing Off

Picture this: A hostile and resistant teenager is slumped on the sofa staring at the TV. You sit down next to him, put your arm around him, tell him you love him (like he believes that), and ask if he's okay and if he wants to talk. Sorry, but that will probably make him pull further away and resent you even more.

Luckily, there are ways that you can let your new stepchildren know that you are a good listener without getting in their faces. We hope you have done a lot of communicating and reaching out prior to the marriage. If you have, the children should already have a feel for what kind of person you are (though their perception might not be positive). How you relate to them *before* marriage can help change their possibly negative perceptions and reservations. After you're married, they may find new reasons to dislike you. They may realize you're a permanent fixture in the house. Or maybe they fear that you will leave them. (Although it may feel to you like, *"Oh no, she's still here."*)

Whatever the reason for lack of initial harmony, tread lightly and gently, and with an understanding step. Are we telling you to tolerate abusive and negative behavior directed toward you? Of course not. But again, do not make everything about you, your needs, and your new position as "mom" in the home. If you want your needs to be met ultimately, you must learn the art of patience and maturity with children who have issues. Also, try these techniques:

- Don't "dig in" to their problem areas with advice and platitudes. Be sincere in your efforts to reach out to them because they will know in a heartbeat if you are doing this for them or just to please their father.
- Try not to attack every behavior or misstep that angers you. Choose your battles and determine with your husband what things to address in a more emphatic way and ignore as much as you can initially.
- You can let them know you are there if they need you, and you would be glad to listen to anything they have to share. Then be observant but don't smother and hover.
- A smile goes a long way in touching needy young children or sullen teenagers.

Above all, respect their space and need for adjustment. Things take time, and if you let them know you are receptive to them and their problems or concerns, eventually you may find you're slowly building a strong relationship.

Redirect Negative Thinking

Focusing on the negative affects people of all ages in myriad ways. Your stepchildren may have many disparaging thoughts, not only about their parents' divorce, but also about issues related to school, friendships, and themselves. Sadly, feelings of negativity or unhappiness can permeate a child's life. Changing children's negative thinking can be a formidable challenge for parents, but you can succeed with focused efforts and adherence to some basic techniques.

Experts know that thoughts cause feelings and feelings cause behaviors. It is therefore difficult, if not impossible, to think positively yet feel negatively in the same moment. So you want your stepchildren to replace their negative thoughts with positive ones. Here are some useful techniques in changing children's thinking, feelings, and behaviors:

- Pay close attention to the child's thinking patterns. Address any "thinking errors" you notice by using these kinds of statements: "I'm thinking Billie wasn't really angry at you. He was just too busy and upset with his own world," or "Okay, so you got a C on your paper. Let's look at it. The good news is that we can learn a lot from it." Discover if the negative thinking is restricted to just a few issues ("I hate when I get an answer wrong in class!") or whether it has become generalized ("I hate my life").

- While a child vents about a certain frustration, listen only long enough to understand the issue. By so doing, you can avoid reinforcing continued negative thinking.
- Be careful not to reinforce negative statements with negative comments of your own.

The good news is that most negative statements, when not reinforced, disappear over time.

Avoid Being Negative Yourself

As you listen to your stepchildren talk about what's bothering them, refrain from comments like, "You shouldn't feel that way" or, "Don't think like that." Also, avoid scolding them: "I'm sick and tired of your whining, complaining, and negativity. Knock it off!" This type of confrontation not only models *negative* thinking, but actually makes the situation worse because you're telling the child that his feelings are wrong. If you make him question his feelings, he may become confused, think he's stupid for not feeling the "right way," and stop sharing his feelings with you.

Reframe Negative Thoughts

When you hear children's negative descriptions of themselves, their school, friends, and other aspects of their lives, reframe them into a positive construction of each issue. By so doing, you implant new ways of thinking. For example, a comment such as, "Boy, I bet you learned a lot from that" will usually elicit a positive response, which you can reinforce and, thus, render more permanent in their psyches. Even though the experience may have been temporarily unpleasant or painful, the child can learn from it.

On the other hand, a simple comment like, "I understand why you might feel that way" validates the child's feeling or right to feel in some way. Next, be sure to reconstruct the issue with the positive expectation that the situation will improve over time.

Reinforce What's Good and Be Patient

Always recognize, reinforce, and affirm any spontaneous positive statements, conversation, or behaviors that your step-kids exhibit as implicit in the expression, "Catch the child being good." When you offer positive comments, you'll encourage the child to have positive thoughts of his own.

We are not attempting to oversimplify a process that requires time, effort, and practice. Changing how a child views life is no small task—it takes strength of character and effort. Your work will pay off, though—your sincere and devoted approach to a positive lifestyle will be far-reaching and will greatly impact your stepchild's future.

Children are not born with anger and negativity; they acquire it through life experiences. Keeping that in mind, recognize the importance of your being an agent in bringing about positive change. It doesn't happen in a day, so we remind you again: patience is one of life's greatest gifts and virtues.

Model Positive Behavior

Be sure to model positive thinking yourself. Searching for and discovering the positives in your own life has a way of attracting more and more positive happenings for you and for those around you. Make no mistake, kids notice and model from how you process and react to your own experiences.

Here are some examples of positive versus negative approaches to requests and advice giving.

Negative	Positive
"Stop running through the house."	"Please walk through the house."
"Don't let go of the monkey bars. Don't fall."	"Hang on tight to the monkey bars!"
"Try not to get into trouble at school again today. Stop disrupting the class."	"I know you'll have a great day at school, and I can't wait to hear about it at dinner."
Starting conversations with "I can't" and "I don't"	Starting conversations with "I can" and "I do"

Seek Out Their Interests and Sources of Pride

As we discussed in Chapter 1, nurturing a child's interests can pay dividends for both of you. This is especially true with children who are shy or having difficulty accepting the new stepfamily.

I (Dr. Wenck) once saw a very oppositional new client, a fourteen-year-old girl. Before my meeting with the girl, her mother told me in confidence, "She's just not going to talk to you." I asked the mother what her daughter most liked to do. The mom replied, "Well, the usual stuff that teenagers are into, but she's nuts about that African gray parrot of hers."

I then invited the daughter into the therapy office to talk privately. She indeed appeared very sullen and resistant. Her first responses to surface questions were "Yes," "No," and "I don't know." Then I asked her if she had any pets. Her eyes brightened immediately as she began to talk excitedly about her bird: his name, where she got him, how old he was, and—most important—his personality. She indicated that sometimes he was "stubborn" and would sometimes "just clam up." We talked a little about why her parrot might be stubborn and silent. You may realize where this is going. Over time, she came to realize that she was really talking about herself. And then the real therapy began.

Like this girl, kids who are initially resistant or hesitant to embrace someone new in their life may come around when they see that person is interested in them and the things they take pride in. Yes, it takes time, but it is so satisfying to witness their pleasure in sharing their personal interests with you. It leads to the child thinking, "Gee, if she's *that* interested in what I like doing, she must like me a little bit. Maybe I should give her a shot." This is positive thinking!

Refer back to page 13 for ideas on how to nurture a child's interests. Children with low self-confidence especially benefit from having someone encourage and support their interests. Approach it as a fun activity. It can engender a stepchild's lifelong sense of gratitude.

Practice Selective Self-Disclosure

Self-disclosure is revealing some aspect of your personal self to another person. So why disclose—particularly to stepchildren? The benefits of self-disclosure are that:

- It is a way of learning more about the other person. When one person discloses, the other tends to do likewise.
- It deepens mutual trust. We become more emotionally intimate with the other person.
- Disclosers feel better when others accept what they say. Getting stuff off the chest is healing. Also, sometimes kids are under the wrong impression that what they might have done or said was awful, when actually it might have been trivial.

- People are seen as more genuine when they disclose both strengths and weaknesses. Self-disclosure increases mutually positive feelings.

When meeting a new person, our talk is at first pretty impersonal—the weather, where you live, the job, the big game, and so on. Recently, I (Dr. Wenck) saw a personable and professional man aboard a flight to Houston, Texas. The young man sat on my immediate right. I initiated conversation by asking, "Visiting friends in Houston?" The response was, "No, I'm seeing one of my company's clients. I'm with a consulting company. And you?" The next level of conversation involved details of vocations and families. Following this were more intimate disclosures by each party regarding their family and marital situations.

This is typical of the progression from surface facts to personal revelations and more intimate issues. Disclosure can include facts, thoughts, feelings, aspirations, goals, failures, successes, fears, dreams, likes, dislikes, and favorites. Both you and the other party can choose to relate your deepest hopes and fears or maintain social distance by staying with relatively impersonal material.

Risks of Self-Disclosure

As with almost anything that has the power for good, disclosure can also have negative effects if used improperly. Realize that not all persons, including stepchildren, will respond in a positive way to your disclosures at a particular point in time. You may even risk later being exploited or embarrassed, as the other party could take advantage of the new information you have supplied. Lastly, certain information may simply not be age-appropriate for young listeners.

Keep in mind that you should use active listening (as detailed in Chapter 1), with attention to what the discloser is really saying and feeling. This, too, can be used effectively with the shy, resistant, or special child. Again, all of us want to be understood, not just listened to.

Tips for Using Self-Disclosure to Your Advantage

We have mentioned the benefits and risks of disclosing personal information to others. Here are some guidelines for using disclosure effectively:

- Know that using disclosure is an art and takes practice. Focus on attentiveness and timing the flow of this complex interaction.
- Attend closely to the "emotional temperature" of the listener. The child may not want to participate at that point in time. Honor that.
- Don't reveal too much too soon. Those who prematurely "dump everything" or bare their soul can make people want to run for cover.
- Use vocabulary that kids understand.
- Take care that disclosing your mistakes or certain negative incidents does not destroy the listener's trust in you.

Also, realize that you may not see the immediate effects of self-disclosure on your relationship with your stepchild (you may not have a teary Hallmark hug). But know that you are building a solid foundation for a healthy bond.

Use Metaphoric Stories

Imagine driving to your grandmother's house, taking the usual route. Suddenly, you come upon a huge fallen tree blocking your way. The crew removing the debris reports that it will be three hours before the road is again clear. They suggest a detour requiring six extra miles, but only thirty minutes of time. Logically, you would choose the detour and go the extra six miles to save 2½ hours of time and frustration.

Taking alternate routes can save time and frustration with stepchildren as well. Parents and stepparents are so often insistent on going directly to the heart of the problem and solving it "right now." But the stepchild with the problem may not want to "go there" right now. Here is an example of how frustration can be avoided and time can be saved by taking an alternate route.

Suppose your fifteen-year-old stepson is angry at his father, who denied his request to go out with two older friends known to drink alcohol. Your attempt to help by talking directly about the issue only makes him furious at you, too. He refuses to talk about it. So the direct route is blocked. But an alternate route could pay dividends if you related a real-life story like this:

"Years ago, when my cousin Sarah was sixteen, she had her heart set on going to a party after a football game with a couple of older girls who would drink beer a friend bought for them. My uncle had serious concerns about the older girls and said no. She got very angry, went to her room, and slammed the door. My uncle tried to reason with her, but she simply clammed up. The next morning she saw pictures and a story on the front page of the newspaper about the same girls, who, after leaving a party, were involved in a serious accident due to drunk driving. They were hospitalized for weeks. The driver was charged with DUI. The other walks with a limp to this day. We were all stunned."

In the heat of emotion, kids often refuse to talk about the actual incident that involves them. However, they will frequently identify with and talk about similar incidents in which *other* individuals were involved, provided they are presented with "safe" differences in gender, age, time, location, or situation. Those characteristics make the stories seem external to them and more comfortable to talk about. By relating to these "outside" events, stepchildren are actually projecting their own thinking and feelings into the story, but they are not aware of it. Issues involving other child/adult clashes can be processed in this way. This technique is referred to variously as using metaphoric stories, the back-door approach, or taking an alternate route.

Use Exercise to Help Kids Cope

Physical and mental health experts frequently recommend exercise in combating a long list of emotional and physical disorders. Pick up any article or book that speaks to obesity, low self-esteem, cardiac issues, depression, aggression, diabetes, anxiety, or insomnia, and exercise will be strongly suggested as a therapeutic technique. Wellness clinics specialize in nurturing optimal physical and mental health rather than just combating disease. These agencies also embrace physical exercise as a core strategy. Clearly, exercise is a most effective method in promoting health. It's great for kids. Why? Because exercise:

- Has been long known to release endorphins into the neurological system, producing feelings of well-being.
- Raises body temperature, which in turn, reduces muscle tension.
- Redirects attention outward, thus reducing anxiety.
- Increases muscle tone, bone strength, and coordination, resulting in enhanced self-esteem.
- Improves blood circulation and breathing activity.
- Provides a healthy outlet for anxiety and aggression.

Convinced yet? We know of no better or quicker vehicle to dissipate and alleviate tension, anger, and resentment than a variety of physical activities. Development of specific athletic skills promotes a sense of pride as well. The list includes sports such as tennis, swimming, basketball, football, and soccer. Try bringing the whole family to an exercise center, where trained professionals can give you suggestions. Assess the children's special interests in this area and explore local opportunities for participation and training.

Follow Your Own Advice

Remember that if exercise is good for kids, it's good for step-moms and dads, too. For those inevitable stressful times, head for the gym or out for a walk.

Shy Children

For combinations of reasons, certain children may be painfully shy. When in a social gathering with stronger or more outgoing personalities, these kids could be miserable and would rather be almost anywhere else. But even celebrities have overcome childhood shyness and self-consciousness. Let's look at four helpful strategies: demonstration, focusing thoughts outward, role-playing, and social practice.

Demonstration

Most kids learn more from a demonstration than just verbal instruction. If your stepchild has acknowledged being shy in certain social situations, you might suggest that he or she watch how you or your new husband handles that kind of situation. For example, let's say you must meet unfamiliar people at a graduation party or other social gathering. Let the child watch how you greet that person, initiate conversation, and respond to make the other party feel at ease. If the child asks how you did that, explain specifically what you said and did.

Focusing Thoughts Outward

People are self-conscious around others if they are overly concerned with how others see them. There is an antidote, however, that works wonders—transferring thoughts and attention to the other person or group.

Let's say your stepchild is worried about that class presentation he has to make next week. You could suggest that he speak directly to one or more of his classmates to help ease into his presentation. For example, if the speech is about basketball history, he could try statements like these to engage his classmates: "Now, we know that Jim here is super at making free throws. And Cathy is great at making threes." This technique nicely establishes lines of communication and personalizes his speech. Plus, his classmates will be pleased to receive this sort of attention. Your stepson will see and feel the effect of their excitement. He then will be much more relaxed and be effectively "out of his own head," which is where his uneasy thoughts are. Self-consciousness will then miraculously disappear.

Role-Playing

Role-playing can be effective as a learning technique to help alleviate shyness. For example, suggest that your stepdaughter imagine that you are that girl or boy she would like to talk to. Use role-playing to illustrate how to start conversations, such as making casual remarks on things they have in common—a certain school subject, the next high school game, the Olympics, unusual weather, and so on. Switch roles on occasion in practicing a variety of situations.

Social Practice

Like anything else, practice brings improvement. Suggest that your shy stepchild deliberately initiate conversation with persons such as the cashier at the grocery store, the post office employee, the clerk at the convenience store, or anyone else with whom they might be in contact during a typical day. Following the strategy of focusing thoughts outward, suggest that they notice and comment on something positive or attractive about that person. This may be their dress, a physical feature, and/or how they do their job. Most usually, the other person will be pleased and make a remark, leading to further conversation. In so doing, tension dissipates and the child gains confidence.

Understanding the Child with Special Needs

Each of us obviously has our own needs and unique qualities and characteristics that make us who we are. Children who are said to have "special" needs, however, may present you with a challenging set of requirements as well as incredible gifts. "Special needs" can cover many categories, from minimal to moderate to severe:

- **Physical disabilities or health conditions:** Food allergies, asthma, diabetes, epilepsy, or severe illnesses
- **Neurological disabilities:** ADHD, autism, Asperger's syndrome
- **Intellectual disabilities:** Learning disorders

- **Mental disabilities:** Various mental-retardation syndromes
- **Emotional disabilities:** Behavioral or emotional handicaps

Your first step should be to avail yourself of any and all resources and information about the child's specific condition, syndrome, or situation. Parenting a child with special needs takes much knowledge and patience with regard to school, home, and daily life in general. A good starting point is *Breakthrough Parenting for Children with Special Needs: Raising the Bar of Expectations* by Judy Winter.

Your relationship with the birth mom is critical in these situations. In the best interest of the child, you need to find out exactly what approach to parenting is successful and what your new stepchild's medical needs may be. What schedule and regimen of care has been effective? Lean on your friends for help and support. Find local support groups led by professionals. Make sure you are connected with the school the child attends as well as physicians, counselors, and all related personnel.

Obviously, the degree of severity of a disability or handicap and its medical ramifications may affect your family life, so if you have children of your own, you'll need to communicate the stepchild's situation to them. Educating your own children on what to expect is very important.

A child with special needs can challenge your patience and understanding. You are one extra and pivotal person in the child's life now, who can provide love, structure, and stability. And what a wonderful gift and learning tool a special-needs child can be for you! Sue M. married a man with custody of his son with Down syndrome. "At first, I was very hesitant and unsure of what my role would be in this little one's life. I read everything I could about Down syndrome and went to his school to meet everyone. He has the sweetest nature and the purest heart. He's made me a better person, and I'm so lucky to have him in our life."

Knowledge and understanding are the best tools for a peaceful and productive home life. You might find this child is also the greatest of gifts.

A Case in Point:
Knowing Their Interests Pays Dividends

At a residential treatment center for troubled children and youth where I (Dr. Wenck) worked, a doctoral intern in psychology brought a thirteen-year-old boy to my office. The intern was highly frustrated because this young man simply refused to talk to anyone or perform any of his responsibilities that day. I later learned that the boy was angry because someone had suspended a favorite privilege due to misbehavior on his part.

Both the intern and I knew in advance that this particular young man was particularly passionate about three issues: (1) his younger brother, (2) riding his bicycle, and (3) getting a new dog. I asked the boy to close his eyes, then led him through a progressive relaxation exercise. When it was obvious that he was deeply relaxed, I suggested that he visualize himself and his little brother riding bicycles to the pet store to get a new dog. Almost immediately, the boy became visibly reflective and content. A smile spread over his face. When he opened his eyes, he was talkative, cooperative, and composed. He had been rescued from the negative thinking that had made him silent and sullen.

That's the power of knowing a child's interests! This boy went from stubborn to relaxed in a matter of moments.

REFLECTIONS: KEY ISSUES IN CHAPTER 2

- Know that resistant and shy children nearly always have understandable reasons for acting that way.

- While the kids may express anger toward you, the real basis for it was probably there long before you.

- Strive to understand difficult issues and reframe them in a positive way.

- Discovering and participating in shy or resistant kids' interests and passions shows your caring and attention to them.

- When frustrated and out of sorts, physical outlets work wonders for kids, you, and their father.

- Disclosing aspects of yourself to kids makes you appear more human and deepens the bond between you.

- Demonstrations, focusing outward, role-playing, and social practice all help to evaporate shyness.

- Helping kids with special-needs requires some research on their situation.

Chapter 3

Establishing Yourself as a New Couple

"Daddy and this lady are really married? Who is this woman? She's the one who stole him from my mom! And now from us? I'm not doing anything she says." To avoid this nightmarish situation, ask yourself the following questions. Have the kids been fully informed? Were they a part of the planning? Have misconceptions on their part been resolved? Unless their questions have been addressed, they just may not accept the new couple as authority figures or models of communication, cooperation, or givers of affection.

Accepting You and Daddy as an Entity

Chances are that from the time they were little, your step-children viewed their parents as one, or as a combined force: "Mom and Dad," "my parents." Most likely, this union was the center of the family unit, and even though the marriage may not have been a good one, it represented stability and home. Divorce and/or death, as hard as it is for children, may not be nearly as difficult as accepting their father as an entity with someone else—in this case, you. They may resent you being on the scene. Unless you have had lots of time to prepare them and communicate with them, they may even blame you for their parents not being together, especially if their father divorced their birth mother. Even in the most turbulent of homes, children notoriously want their parents to stay together. Now, they are faced with their father and his wife—their stepmom.

Communication Is Key

Before you get married, be sure that you and your partner facilitate discussions, communication, and even counseling so that the children understand that you are not there to take their mother's place. You are there because you love their father and want to be a life partner with him. Separate these two notions.

Your love for their father and his commitment and devotion to you are the exact example you want to set for these children. You need to demonstrate the emotional connection you have and that you love each other unconditionally. That is what marriage should be, and that is what you should display to them. Do not exclude them, but give them time to observe a healthy relationship and what a commitment between husband and wife looks like.

Try an opener like this: "Nick and Emma, you know that your dad and I have been dating for two years. Well, we have some exciting news! In six months, we're going to get married! I am really looking forward to becoming a full-time part of your life. Please know that I'm not replacing your mom. I just want to be another caring person. Nor am I taking your father from you. He loves you more than ever right now, and I know that he will continue to do so."

In every single instance when we talked with women who felt they had a successful second marriage that included stepchildren, their response was the same: "I never doubted that he put me first." Your husband must put you first unconditionally, the same as you must put him first. There are no exceptions. This does not mean that he cannot have a relationship with his children, talk to them privately, or maintain his commitment to them. If you have a small baby at home, for example, it often needs immediate attention, and it's your responsibility to take care of that. Putting your spouse first does *not* mean that you put the baby aside, tell him he has to wait, and tend to every whim of your spouse when he walks in the door. Putting your spouse first means that you make life decisions together, live by certain standards, and keep your word. You both always take into consideration the feelings and needs of the other.

The Adjustment Period

Before you and your new spouse got together, his kids most probably had one set of adults to care about them. Now you, the stepmom have been added. Should their birth mom remarry, the kids would have two sets of adults to teach them and meet their needs. For many reasons, this can be a big plus.

As your new family learns to trust each other, the example of love, trust, and commitment should extend to the children. Rather than viewing you as a threat or interloper, the children will learn to respond to your demonstration of love and caring for them. You can fill a role in their lives as a loving and caring adult and friend. Form a team with your husband and let the children know that you, too, care for them and are willing to provide them with the love and consideration they need and deserve when they are with you.

Patience Is Key

We can't stress enough the importance of patience with your stepchildren. So many stepmoms told us they just expected everything to "work out" and everyone to fall into the mom, dad, and kid roles. While the honeymoon period can be brief (if it even happens at all), eventually you can develop into a family unit when the children learn to trust you and see that your feelings for them are sincere.

Keep in mind that kids are wired differently than adults. Things that you think should be obvious might not be to them. You are the adult; keep telling yourself that. Also, learn not to be too hard on yourself when you find it difficult to love or even like your stepkids.

Keep your expectations at a realistic level. Relationships develop when kids are given time to trust you. Set goals for your family and yourself and teach by example. But remember, you'll probably be silently counting to ten more often than you thought. (Hopefully not forever.)

Establishing Your Authority

When the kids see you and your husband as an entity, it will be easier to accept that both of you are the authority figures and share equally in setting the household expectations and guidelines. If your husband has lived alone with his children for a while, or even if he has visitation rights only, it becomes easy for the children to see themselves and their dad as the only possible members of the family unit. They may have had an arrangement that worked for them, and now here you are to mess things up. Emerge slowly as an isolated authority figure—first be sure to let them view the two of you as a unit. When they totally understand that the two of you are the adults, the caretakers, and that you provide a united front, it will be easier to accept your position in the family.

Again, lots of communication, combined with patience, respect, and understanding, are needed. You cannot arrive on the scene and start dictating. You may be used to giving orders and setting standards in your previous situation, but merging two families takes much compromise. You and your husband have the responsibility to set up the family structure, but please remember to be as subtle and supportive as you can, especially in the beginning. Figure out where the kids are coming from and what they are used to, and then set your goals.

How to Handle Certain Situations as a Team

As you and your husband establish yourself as a united front to the children, you'll likely run into some common scenarios. Here are some of those, along with tips on how to deal with each particular one.

Communication

Consistent communication from both parents is often a skill that takes a while to establish even under the best of circumstances. You may be a great communicator in your own right but feel totally disabled when it comes to approaching new children, and talking to teenagers in particular. No matter how *hard* you try to communicate on their level, they may refuse to open up and share their feelings. Relax. That's often the case with teens, whether they are your biological children or not. The important thing is to explain your feelings and your expectations and to let them know you are always open to listening to them. Being fair is often hard, and hearing that *you* are not being so can be very troubling for you.

Remember that you and your husband are working together, not alone, and the two of you can approach every issue together. This is not to say that there are never times when you each interact and communicate with the children on an individual level, but if they know the two of you are a team, neither parent is compromised. Let's say that Zach is having trouble with algebra. After talking with Zach to see what he thinks, the biological parent (in this case, let's say it's Dad) should go to the school to visit with Zach's math teacher as well as Zach's counselor. That way, Dad can learn more about the specific issues and report back. Say the teacher and counselor suggest that Zack get a tutor. At this point, you could offer to step in and do some research on the school's list of available tutors to find someone. The biological parent(s) should make the final decision (your husband may wish to confer with Zach's mother). But all through this, you can be helpful and supportive, offering whatever service and input your partner thinks is beneficial.

Resolving Conflict

Conflict resolution tactics are universal: identify the problem, set a realistic resolution or goal, identify each person's role and responsibility, and determine what each person is willing to do to solve the conflict. Kids have rights as well as you do, and even though you are the parents, be sure to listen to their issues and concerns, and (here we go again) be fair. Put a plan in writing if necessary, and have those involved sign it. This often works with younger children better than teenagers. Once you have the plan, you as the parents have to decide on consequences if one or the other breaks their part of the bargain.

You might have a situation like this: There are three children in your home most weekends. There is one television on which a Wii console is attached. Of course, everyone wants to use the Wii at the same time. Conflict breaks out. Here's how conflict resolution could work:

1. You, your partner, and children schedule a group meeting to get the problem specifics.
2. You and your partner draw up a rough draft of a plan for equal usage. Present it to the children for their input.
3. Implement the final plan, explaining that it will be reviewed in two weeks for needed modifications.
4. Modify the plan as needed and continue.

If the conflict is with *you*—and this may be the case—you can do your best to compromise and work out an equitable resolution with which everyone can live. Sometimes, as we know, life isn't fair, and there may be times when the bottom line has to be decided by you and your husband as the responsible adults.

Bestowing Affection

Can you and your husband display affection for one another? Absolutely. Of course, remember that you are responsible adults and should never carry on in a way that would make another person in the room uncomfortable. Be discreet. Your love and respect for one another can be demonstrated in many ways as well—how you speak to one another and the consideration you display, for example.

By all means, show your new stepchildren affection as well—within the limits of their comfort zones. Respect personal space and take the time to determine what they need from you. Some children take a long time to trust and warm up to a newcomer. Knowing them and their personalities and personal preferences can help you decide how much overt affection they require. Maybe you are the touchy-feely type yourself, but you can show affection in many different ways. The important thing is to gauge their needs and what makes them feel loved and comfortable.

Do not barge in, "glomming" onto children, until your role as stepmom is established and you become familiar with each other. Little children will probably be more accepting of overt affection than teenagers, especially in the beginning. It's easier to let them come to you in their own time. Kind words, considerate acts, and personalized notes go a long way in showing someone you care for them and you want to be there for them.

Be Relationship Role Models

To foster love or, at least, acceptance, you have to keep mutual respect at the forefront of every interpersonal relationship in the family. You and your husband will set the tone for the relationships that you will develop with the children. That's why the two of you as an entity will strongly determine the harmony and success of this new family you are building.

Conflicts among the children are a lot easier to resolve than any complaint they may have with you. Act like parents and decide the guidelines as well as the consequences for the children. If you teach and model the rule of "treating others like you wish to be treated," they can never come back and say, "Well, that's not what *you* do." Be sure you and your husband show each other respect and affection and solve your disagreements maturely and fairly.

Keep Your Relationship Strong

Besides the other thousand things you and your husband need to do as you blend your families, you two, as a new couple, should identify and specify certain needs and goals for yourselves. Consider the following common needs in all marriages.

Your Need for Privacy

Couples need private time to deal only with each other apart from business, family, and social responsibilities. Your quest is to learn to respond to, understand, and connect with each other, and yet preserve your individual personalities. A healthy identity as a couple first requires clear and distinct individual identities. Follow these steps to establish a positive identity as a couple:

1. Let the children and family members know that you will need consistent and regular private time together.
2. Plan these times in advance, whether they might include evenings out, weekend vacations, or romantic dinners at home or at your favorite venues. List them on the family calendar.
3. Activate the plan. Make it a priority. A strong couple is the foundation of a strong stepfamily.

Your Need for Intimacy

Humans do not flourish without intimacy, connection, bonding, and attachment. Mental health experts agree that it is wonderfully therapeutic to be deeply understood and accepted. For this to develop, couples need physical, intellectual, and emotional intimacy. This process is hampered when others are constantly underfoot and "need" you 24/7. To help nurture intimacy, consider these ideas:

- When your bedroom door is closed, tell others to knock or call one of your cell phones instead of barging in.
- Keep your passionate displays of affection private.
- When the kids are around, dress appropriately. This is not Victoria's Secret time.
- Be aware of sexual emergence on the part of adolescents (see Chapter 9).
- Adolescent males and females can and do develop attractions for the nonbiological parent.
- Keep your romance alive with regular alone time.

The glow of romance quickly dims when excessive attention is paid to work, other family members, friends, and social obligations. So often this occurs with individuals who are excessively achievement oriented. It is as if they inwardly say, "Now that I'm married, I've got to get back to business." In fact, nurturing your romance and relationship needs is a big part of that "business."

Your Need for Romance

Researchers have long agreed that *romantic* love—which they state is based heavily upon physical attraction—usually transforms into *companionate* love—composed of long-term intimacy and commitment. Some who read about the romantic/companionate issue may become slightly disenchanted. For example, they may come to view the long-term companionate phase as passionless and dull. Yet nothing could be further from the truth. Partners who keep an open mind can continue to deepen their mutual love, and as a result, certain positive traits, not noticed at first, begin to emerge and develop.

Romance, intimacy, and the deepening of positive feelings do not develop automatically. You must continue nurturing them by sensitive, caring interactions. We are aware of no better handbook than the highly regarded *1001 Ways to Be Romantic,* by Greg Godek, long-time romantic seminar leader. Here are excerpts of some of Godek's ideas:

- Romance is all about attitude. The right attitude can make cleaning the garage romantic. The wrong attitude can turn a romantic dinner into a diet struggle.
- Listen well with your ears, mind, and heart. Listen particularly, for the feeling behind the words.
- Write love notes to him or her! Compose a song or poetry. Leave affectionate messages or voice mails.
- Get some gifts, such as jewelry, candy, flowers, love coupons, invitations for dinner, theatre tickets, and more. Place them in each other's workbag, suitcase, car seat, and elsewhere. Who cannot be moved by such thoughtful and symbolic gestures?

Notice that Godek suggests both attitudinal approaches as well as specific positive actions. Use his ideas or your own creativity to reignite and/or keep the glow in your relationship. The more you practice such techniques, the more adept you become. Don't be satisfied with just being average. Go for the best relationship in town!

Financial Issues and Goals

We'll talk about financial issues and related pitfalls in a few places in this book, since money matters are so crucial to the health of relationships. Here, we'll talk about specific suggestions particularly crafted for the new couple.

You two must agree on your financial goals. If you and your partner do not have a clear idea of where you want to get financially, you might end up somewhere else. How do you want to live in five years? Ten years? At retirement? Perhaps, on a more basic level, it is well to consider why you want to be financially successful. One's motivations as to why we wish this or that success is, again, quite revealing as to our approach to life in general.

Now that it is the eleventh hour, do you know the status of both of your money matters? Good problem-solving approaches involve starting where you are *now*. 'Tis a far, far better thing to know the facts now than to be surprised later. As with other aspects of character, it all too often happens that the passion of a new relationship may cloud the inconvenient truths of questionable monetary track records. Owing to a singular such negative experience, one of our stepmoms, when asked what prospective stepmoms should know about their guy before marriage, virtually shouted, "Get a credit report and a background check!"

You may know what your beloved's income and assets may be, but do you know his obligations? Another stepmom-to-be recently found, to her dismay—during the second year of their relationship—that her fiancé owed the IRS $140,000 in back taxes. We rest our case.

Engage in Full Financial Honesty

It's essential that you and your partner openly list both your individual financial assets and obligations. Determine your combined strategies for eliminating indebtedness. Interestingly, one's financial track record reveals a good deal about the broader aspects of his or her character. Some have told us that they see one's credit rating as such a marker. Accountants are said to have quite an in-depth knowledge of the nature of their clients as individuals. Ideally, the new couple should be a team pulling together with similar values. Following is an example of two partners who are not on the same page:

Angel is the accountant of the family, who balances the books and budget. "We took care of our monthly bills, got our credit cards paid down, put $100 into our new joint IRA, and had $18 to spare." New husband Bob jubilantly hops into the room and reports, "Honey, I just bought another boat. Couldn't pass it up. Got a great deal on it. Can you work it out?"

Consider the Cost of Kids' Pre-College Education

Knowledge is empowering. This section poses the kinds of questions you and your husband should consider regarding your kids' educational needs and expenses. Chapter 13 lists specific strategies to address these needs. At this point, we strongly suggest that you get accurate answers to the following critical questions and issues as soon as possible:

1. Do you wish public or private education for the elementary- and high school–age children?
2. What are the comparative expenses for each type of schooling, including tuition, books, transportation, and extracurricular activities?
3. Whose obligation, according to divorce decree or subsequent court orders, is it to fund these expenses? To what degree?

Plan for College

What are the post–high school educational plans for each child? Huge differences exist between the yearly tuition expense at a local junior college, technical training institutes, out-of-state institutions of higher learning, and elite private universities such as Harvard and Princeton. Some states do not allow the inclusion of language in a divorce decree regarding parental obligation of their children's college expenses. This can produce unwelcome surprises, as either biological parent can then legally abdicate responsibilities for the college education expenses of the children.

Your Personal Goals as a Stepmom

You are, or are about to become, a wife and stepmom. Perhaps you're already a mom. You want to be a crucial part of this newly created family. You're excited about this process and want all to go well. You give of yourself to your spouse, his kids, your kids, mutual relatives, and friends to make it happen. Maybe you're running around meeting everyone's needs but yours? Sound familiar?

Trying to be all things to all people, by the way, is the shortest route to burnout. Remember who you are. Who was that lady your new husband or fiancé fell in love with? What had you come to respect about yourself? Don't lose your own identity and individuality in an attempt to meet the needs of the masses. Children ultimately need to learn and grow and be able to meet their own needs independently.

What are your own goals as an individual? What have you always wanted to learn, to see, and to experience? Have you put these desires too long on hold? You can help others more effectively by being an honest, interesting, and well-rounded model who is on the way to fulfilling herself. Keep on learning and share that which you learn. Obviously, we're not suggesting that you use resources for yourself that rightfully belong to another. Quite frankly, if you're reading this book, we don't think you are doing so.

Revisit your own personal short- and long-range goals. Write them down. Perhaps your goals may include unique experiences and/or learning a new skill. Make your goals your passion. Clarify them. Be specific as to amount, degree, shape, manner, or whatever descriptors are appropriate. Visualize yourself in the act of accomplishing these goals. Remember, a healthy and happy you is inherently a better mom and stepmom.

His Personal Goals

Your partner will also need to identify, clarify, visualize, and pursue his specific goals. You can be a catalyst for change in your partner's life. Note the times when he flashes that sparkle you know and love. It may have to do with that new trip or an experience he's always wanted. Reinforce those moments of insight when he may be rethinking a goal that has long been on the shelf. Help him to devise a strategy for achieving dreams that he may have abandoned. Facilitate his efforts. It will pay you dividends. Have him read the above section, "Your Personal Goals as a Stepmom." They apply to him as well.

Planning for an "Ours," Perhaps?

So many considerations, potential benefits, and caveats relate to the decision to bring a new baby into the picture. An entire book could be written on this subject alone. The major issues include the following.

Why Do You Wish to Have Another Child?

Moms and stepmoms tell us, "It's just natural to want to have a child of your own flesh and blood." This is understandable, of course. The key is to be sure that *both* of you clearly want this. So often, one partner does and the other does not or is indecisive about it. Legitimate reasons exist for both. You may have one or more children of your own, but he has none. Or vice versa. One of you may have already "been there and done that" with the diapers and 2 A.M. feedings. You or he may simply wish to get on with life.

No matter what, we suggest that this decision be made for the right reasons—that you both truly want this new addition to your family. It's not fair to expect the newborn to solve existing problems. Yes, babies can and often do aid in bringing stepfamilies together. Common interest in the "new project" may cause residual resentments to evaporate. Beware, though, that if not handled with some finesse, that bundle of joy can generate divisiveness as well.

At any rate, if one or both of you remain reluctant about a new addition, it's best to delay until both of you agree that it's a good thing. For obvious reasons, avoid taking the approach of "After I get him to say 'I do,' I'll get the decision I want." Reputable counseling can help clarify motivations and reservations. Obviously, this is one more of the many decisions that is best resolved *prior* to marriage.

Announcing Your Decision to Others

For many reasons, you should tell his kids and/or your kids that you are considering this step before getting pregnant. This gives them time to mull and digest the potential impact upon them. Their initial reactions may well run the gamut from joyousness to being upset. They may still be recovering from feelings of being displaced or experiencing an unwanted restructuring of their lives.

If your final decision is "go," now comes the finesse part. The children need assurances that the new baby will not subtract from your love and attention to them. Tell them that love can have a way of multiplying rather than dividing. By all means, let them know that their reactions, whatever they are, are understandable and acceptable. Many potential negative reactions can be preempted by up-front assurances like, "We understand that you might be uneasy about this, and we want you to know that you are more important than ever to us. We need your help in this. This is your family, too." Include them in decisions as to preparations, supplies needed, room colors, preferences as to potential names, actual hands-on help with the baby, and more. Be sure they know that you will make final decisions. Ensure that you take some of their suggestions.

Reporting the planning of an addition to the family to exes is the job of the other ex. This includes announcements to extended family members as well. Never have the children share this news. Reassure the ex that existing children will not be diminished in importance or attention.

When the New Baby Arrives

Excitement will be in the air for the well-prepared stepfamily! Each existing child should have an integral part in the process of caring for the new baby, directly or indirectly. This can be an extremely valuable learning experience for them. What better apprenticeship could they have for life than the proper care and feeding of an infant? Despite your attempts to involve each child, one or more may still be reluctant to take part. This is actually not very different from children's reactions in natural families. In either case, you may hear expressions of wanting the new infant to be flushed down the toilet or sent back to "where it came from." If you hear these kinds of comments, ask that child to help in some way with the actual handing of the baby. Even the most stubborn child will likely be won over by a newborn's smiles, giggles, and reactions. After some of these experiences coupled with your praise for their help, we think they'll get hooked.

Now you are both a parent and stepparent. Do not forget your roles and responsibilities in each.

Legal Issues

Necessary legal precautions are easy to forget in the romance and excitement of a marriage. With the new couple, especially in the event of "his, hers, and ours," and/or the anticipation of an "ours," situations can become increasingly complex. New matters of concern include changes in custody, one or both parents moving out of state, new education issues, change of an ex-spouse's situation, your own inheritance issues, new family responsibilities, your financial situation, potential adoption issues, and more.

Keep current with the language and intent of your previously drafted documents. If changes are needed, you may well need the services of an attorney. Seek the advice of friends in selecting an attorney or consult directories listing attorneys who specialize in the area of your need. Make a phone call to the court systems in your county to get advice. Remember, again, that state laws differ widely. You may need help in interpreting the "legalese" of the statutes themselves.

A Case in Point: Saying "No"

Barbara thought she had covered all the bases before marrying her new husband, Frank. He had two teenage daughters with whom she had worked diligently to establish a relationship prior to the marriage. But the girls were used to having their father all to themselves, and Barbara didn't realize how possessive and jealous they were underneath their seemingly friendly and open exterior. They began undermining her and doing subtle things to cause conflict. Frank seemed helpless in the situation, worrying about alienating his daughters, whom he was determined to keep happy and away from the influences of his ex-wife. Barbara also felt that the girls used Frank as a "walking ATM" and were constantly demanding material things. The bank was pretty much open for the girls prior to the marriage. Barbara began feeling she was on an island by herself. Frank's explanation, "If I show the girls too much attention or affection, Barbara gets upset. But if I show Barbara too much attention or affection, the girls get upset," was a red flag for her. Obviously, the girls saw Barbara as an outsider who threatened not only their relationship with their father, but their security as well. Frank couldn't seem to get his own priorities and sense of responsibility in order.

Barbara, determined to keep her marriage together and also not hurt the girls, insisted on some family counseling, starting with her and Frank. Eventually, the girls were included in the sessions and began to open up about their feelings toward their new stepmom. Frank began to realize that his commitment to Barbara was a good thing for the girls to see and a great example to set. He also realized that he was not doing his children any favors by constantly doling out money and giving in to their every whim. Barbara began to be less possessive of Frank, giving him more space and time with the girls. The girls eventually saw their dad and stepmom as a team who, together, were there for the girls and truly loved and cared about them and their welfare. It took a while, but they did manage to come together as a family unit.

The girls are both grown and married, and Frank and Barbara survived the storm. She told us that the oldest daughter recently came to her and said, "Thanks for loving us enough to say 'no' at the right times."

REFLECTIONS: KEY ISSUES IN CHAPTER 3

- Accepting you, the stepmom, and Daddy as an entity is not an easy task for the kids.

- Having you and your husband and their biological mom and a new partner, the kids might well benefit from two sets of adults in nurturing, caring for, and guiding them.

- The kids' acceptance of the new couple's authority is always a work in progress.

- The new couple can be invaluable models of good communication, conflict resolution, affection, and cooperation.

- While the kids have abundant needs, so do you and your husband or fiancé as individuals.

- Specific needs of new couples include privacy, intimacy, romance maintenance, financial security, as well as rational planning for each kid's educational needs.

- Each adult needs to preserve his or her own identity, be involved in selected interests and activities, and cultivate personal friendships.

- If you're considering a new baby, be very sure from the outset that both partners really want it.

- Blending families in any situation occasions the need for legal guidance, interpretations, and decisions. Understand everyone's rights and privileges before negotiation or taking action.

Chapter 4

What's Our Address?

"I'd really rather not live in his house. It's permeated with memories of 'her.' But if we absolutely have to, it'll need a total makeover, with new pictures and decorations. I know his kids will like it when I'm through. We could live in my house, but he might have the same misgivings about that. Maybe we should buy a new house—if we can sell both of ours. We might need a bigger one when all of the kids are with us. We have to think about their schools, too. . . ."

Sound familiar? Deciding where to live is a huge consideration with *lots* of variables. After all, your home is where you're building a foundation for a family. Factors like demographics, size, neighborhood, schools, shopping, proximity to family, and certainly money play a part in the decision-making process. Emotions run deep with children, and their connection to their home is usually strong. Think about whether, and how recently, you have uprooted them already. Custody arrangements and how often his or your combined brood is with you is also something to think about. Are the bedrooms for visiting or ownership? Will this be your permanent residence where the kids return during college

vacations, or a temporary place that just meets your requirements for space at the present? This needs to be *home* for all
of you.

My House or His?

If you have lived in your home for a while, you may have a
strong bond and a need to stay put. On the other hand, you
may have negative or painful associations with it and would
be happy to bid it farewell. If you have children, your house
may represent a security they need, but it may also represent
another "mom and dad" with whom they lived.

The same variables are in place for your new husband.
He may have only recently moved into his present residence
and have no qualms about moving. If he has custody of his
children, chances are this is the house they have been living in for some time. If you can jointly agree to accept one
home or another, the problem of "where" is obviously less
of a stress factor. You might agree to sell both homes, and
start your new family adventure in a totally different home
that belongs to your new family. In any scenario, you need
to establish the "who pays for what" guidelines and what
names go on the deed.

Moving In to His House

If you agree to live in his home, you might have a struggle to make it yours. However, if his home is bigger and can
accommodate all of you, then common sense would dictate
that this is the choice you should make. You don't have to
uproot his children, possibly have them change schools, and
deal with the issues of moving two households. If you can
avoid those changes, great.

But if this is a home where he lived with his ex-wife, can you get past that and make it your own? You are the only person who can answer that question. Of course, your new husband should understand your wish to do at least some redecorating and rearranging to make the residence your own, especially if it was once occupied by his past love. Often, stepmoms who move into the house he and his kids occupy feel like a visitor, or even an alien, for a time. If you have *any* question about doing that successfully, tell your partner now. If you have strong doubts about whether you can live comfortably in his house, you probably shouldn't move there. Your unease will surface over and over.

If he's not living in the home he shared with his ex-wife, it may be less difficult for you to make the decision to live there. But it does *need* to feel like home. Your "address" deserves much discussion, foresight, and consideration. You must be able to start your new marriage in a place that is comfortable and welcoming and where you will not feel like an interloper.

Moving In to Your House

He may have the same issues about moving into your home. In our conversations with stepmoms, we have found that men usually have fewer issues with moving in to your home even if you did previously reside there in another marriage. Perhaps it is because it is the woman who is the "nest-builder." But if he brings his children to your existing home, be very sensitive to any uneasiness they have. If they join you in your home, it needs to become and feel like their home as well. Can you share what has been your space and your things?

A New Abode

Sometimes selling both homes and buying your own together seems to make sense. Then you all start out together, the family map is established, and hopefully the "mom, dad, and kids" roles can develop with fewer territorial issues. Plus, a new home can be exciting for all of you.

Again, you two will have a host of factors to consider when totally starting the homestead over:

- You have to sell or vacate two households instead of one, which is more than twice the workload in actuality.
- You'll both have to deal with utility and insurance companies, real estate transactions, possible remodeling, and address changes.
- You certainly have to consider the financial impact of selling two homes and upgrading to a larger house that accommodates the new family. Will either of you lose money if you sell now? Consider equity, insurance costs, house payment, down payment, repairs, realtor fees, closing costs, and moving costs when you consider selling one or both homes.

Before you make this decision, like it or not, get some input from the other family members.

Asking for the Kids' Input

You and your partner should survey the kids, both his and yours, about where they want to live. Younger children might not be as reluctant to move as older children or teenagers who don't want to leave their friends or their bedrooms and their territory. Get past your own possible insecurities and be sensitive to keeping the changes in their lives to a minimum. Understand that the kids have already had to deal with a number of significant changes and losses.

Sit down together and gauge their feelings and concerns. Consider their needs and ask them what they feel about including new people in their home or moving to another one. In doing so, you may be able to put their fears to rest. If not, at least you listened and validated their feelings as an integral part of the decision-making process. Remember that you and your husband, as the adults, must make the final decision. This, as with any other such issue, is not to be decided by a majority vote.

Be prepared for problems that may arise regardless of your decisions about where to live, and use a mature and sensible approach to conflict resolution. Security is a huge concern for all of you, so keep in mind that you are the adults, and it's your responsibility to provide the kids with a home that is stable, secure, and comfortable. Approach the decision about where to reside as a united front. If one or both of you, as the adults and parents, have reservations, the kids will know, and it can become a nagging source of conflict.

The Physical Structure of the House

One of the first things to consider is the number of children in the new family and whether they all reside with you on a full-time or weekend basis. Kids desperately need their own space, and room for their possessions. Can you find a bedroom for each of them, or are they fine with sharing a room? Some kids don't mind sharing a room, and it might be a bonding experience. Others may object loudly to this arrangement.

Obviously, what you can afford has to be the first consideration. Stretching yourself financially is not a good way to start out your new marriage, but if some extra money spent on housing makes everyone more comfortable, please think about it as a good investment. Waiting for the bathroom when everyone has to go to school and work is a nightmarish way to start the day. You need enough bathrooms so a constant line doesn't form. You really don't want anyone setting his alarm for 4 A.M. just to get a turn in the shower.

You also need to be very aware of your own needs for space and privacy. If you lived alone or even alone with your children, moving into a household with many new people can be very unsettling. You all need room to breathe, and if you feel that you are on top of one another, suffocation will plague all of you. Your home has to have a place the kids can call their own, watch TV, and invite friends over. Make sure there is enough yard space to accommodate young children, in particular, and also any pets you may have. Don't forget space for all the vehicles that your new family will have, too.

There are so many things to think about when considering where you live. We can't stress enough that space, privacy, and comfort should guide your choices. You'll likely have to compromise on some factors. Perhaps you can't buy a brand-new house, but you can find an older one that's larger than you expected. You can always remodel, build on, or restructure in the future if you plan to stay for the long haul.

Temporary Housing

If you must move into a temporary place while you look for a bigger/better home, remember that the less you move and shift people around, the better. If at all possible, keep a timeline on this temporary situation so everyone knows it's a short-term headache.

Proximity to Schools, Shopping, Friends, and More

Above all, if you're choosing a new location, avoid changing schools if at all possible. Older children are usually more impacted by a school change than younger kids. If changing schools is the only option, then at least try to choose a home that is close to the new school, and consider all transportation factors. The kids are facing enough changes—keep their academic life stable if you can.

Keeping the kids close to their friends is also a positive. Kids rely on their friends so much as they get older, and often that seems to be the most important thing in their lives. Yes, they make new friends constantly as they go through life, but keeping them close to their current friends during times of change is really important.

So, Can I Bring My Pet Iguana?

No matter where you live, encountering new pets can be a strange and wonderful experience. Even if you love all animals and become instantly smitten with the kids' ferret, parrot, rabbit, and/or snake, your life will change a bit. Where the new "member(s) of the family" will live, what degree of freedom they are allowed, their personal habits, and necessary care and costs are all issues to be reckoned with. But, of course, you've fully checked out this matter beforehand. That is what courting is all about, right? It's good to be introduced to all new house members in advance. They just might captivate you. By the way, don't parrots typically live to be seventy or eighty years old? You may even need to put them in your will. And how will your chihuahua get along with their pit bull?

With your new family, you will probably be running one child or another to various activities and commitments. Make it as easy on yourself as you can by choosing a home that is close to the things and places your family needs. When your larger family is assembled, a weekly trip to the supermarket can easily turn into every other day. Look around and determine how close you are to the doctor, the vet, the hospital, and church.

Decorating, Redecorating, and Rearranging

"I'm going to make this house my own," you say? Obviously, this is an easier task in a residence that's new for everyone. Still, his kids, your kids, and maybe your husband may well value certain pictures, knickknacks, and pieces of furniture no matter how soiled, weather-beaten, and dog-eared (literally!). These familiar items, for better or worse, allow them to cling to fond memories.

Be patient and understanding. Perhaps Sally wants certain items (like the portrait of her mother) to be placed lovingly in her own bedroom, as opposed to the family room where it once prominently hung. A special note regarding children of deceased biological moms: These children might, understandably, have even deeper needs to keep their mom's memory alive. Tact and patience are the watchwords. Let the kids have special items to display or store in their rooms.

Furniture, too, is a projection of our personality and, as such, has a special meaning to each of us. If anyone in the house has furniture of sentimental value, keep it and find a use for it or consider restoring it. Be sure everyone knows why this item is particularly special.

Make It a Family Affair

It's a great idea to include the kids in the process of decorating, redecorating, or rearranging. You certainly don't need to take all their suggestions, but each one should see one or more of his or her ideas incorporated in the "new design." Taking them with you while searching for items at auctions and outlets becomes a bonding experience all its own.

In-Laws' Approval Needed?

The term "in-law" has been humorously synonymous with "outlaw" in some circles. You may think you and your husband will be the ones to make the decision of where to live, and rightfully so. But your parents and your husband's parents can be very influential and supportive. Grandparents play a critical role in children's lives, and they can also be very concerned and opinionated. No one likes to see their children, of any age, getting a divorce and making huge life changes. It's probably been a painful experience for them if they have played a role of caregiver for their grandchildren. Things that affect their grandchildren are very important to them, and their feelings should not be taken lightly. Mary told us that her husband's parents had grave reservations about him remarrying and moving the children. She said, "I wish I would have been more considerate of their feelings in the beginning. I was just determined that they not interfere with our decisions."

You don't have to let them be an interfering influence on your decision making, but considering their feelings can benefit all of you in the future. Their approval, backing, and assistance can make for a smoother transition as you blend your families. Do your best to include them in your choices for your new home, if only to keep them informed of your decisions. Including them, within *reason*, can be a wise determination for a harmonious lifestyle, since you want them to feel welcome and comfortable in your home.

A Case in Point: Making a House a Home

David was living with his twin daughters in what was the family home when he and Elizabeth decided to marry. Elizabeth became very uncomfortable with the idea of living with her own two young sons in a house that had been what she felt was another woman's. She felt the new family needed to start together in a home that was solely theirs.

She and David found a house in the right neighborhood that they both loved. Unfortunately, the time of sale and purchase was prior to the marriage, and they had agreed not to live together beforehand. David and his daughters moved in six months before Elizabeth and her sons could join them. By the time she got there, David's twins, who were used to living alone with their father, had taken over. Given the circumstances, Elizabeth did not feel like the home was hers. "I really struggled, and I felt like an intruder in what was supposed to be my own home. It took a long time before I could make it work. It just wasn't a good way to start the marriage."

REFLECTIONS: KEY ISSUES IN CHAPTER 4

- Deciding where to live involves many variables and quite a number of people.

- His kids may be more comfortable in his house, but now you are the visitor.

- Are you ready to share your residence and space with everybody?

- A new abode is probably best if it's financially feasible.

- Consider the kids' input in decisions about housing, redecorating, and arranging issues.

- Size, space, and privacy are vital issues to consider.

- Don't forget the pets!

- Convenience and proximity to school, shopping, and friends, are important to everyone.

- Listen, appreciate, but don't be totally governed by extended family members.

Chapter 5

Custody Arrangements with His (and Maybe Your) Kids

Even if you've been dating your partner for years, marriage changes everything. Whereas you might have been Dad's girlfriend or fiancée, who lived somewhere else before, now you're with him all the time—or so it seems to his kids. Coping with the assigned custody arrangements is the new order of the day. The new challenges can seem bewildering. You'll need some planning and preparation to get through it.

Custody arrangements? Let us count the ways. Actually, there are four basic types, each with its own variations. Newly created family units can also play a significant role in how each custody type plays out. What if the biological parents live significant distances apart? Should any children be formally adopted? Do his kids have beloved pets? It's enough to make your head spin.

Defining the Family Unit and Subunits

Before we go any further, let's discuss the many ways a family can take shape.

The Family Unit

We'll define the family unit in the broadest and most inclusive terms. It consists of you, new hubby, his kids, your kids, grandchildren, and grandstepchildren, as well as any and all extended family members such as aunts, uncles, your parents, and his parents. Whether the extended family members are included really depends upon how often they are present for family activities, holidays, birthdays, and other gatherings.

Subunits

Here you have all sorts of combinations. Of course, you and your new husband, as the new couple, constitute one. In all this talk of kids, stepkids, ex-spouses, and extended family members, don't let the couple subunit get swallowed up into one or more of the others. *Protect and preserve its identity, integrity, and continuity.* After all, becoming a couple is the principal reason you married in the first place, right?

Other subunits are defined by their cohesiveness and activity level. They can wax and wane just like any organization. By our definition, they may include:

1. Dad and his kids
2. Dad and your kids
3. You and your kids
4. You and his kids
5. You and/or him with any child, stepchild, grandparent(s), and so on

See how complex and interesting this can get? Right about now, we are reminded of the stepmom satisfaction that Tiffany reported: "I just love having a houseful!"

What Custody Type Do You Have?

There are four basic types of custody, with many variations of each. Please note that your state of residence may employ different terms and definitions for these arrangements. Check out the custody statutes in your state.

Occurring most frequently is some form of *primary custody*. *Full* or *sole custody* is another. Additionally, some form of *joint custody* may be ongoing with his and your kids. Finally, the court may have ordered a type of *split custody*. Let us address each with their respective benefits and shortcomings. Obviously, many of these decisions may have already been made by the time you came into the picture. But as kids get older and situations change, modifications may be needed, so it's useful to know what's what.

Primary Custody

Other names for this form of custody include primary residence, primary care, and physical custody. Generally, this arrangement places the majority of the authority—and responsibility—with the primary custodial parent. In this case, the child(ren) will be living with the custodial parent most of the time.

The benefit of primary custody is that the kids' living situation seems more defined and predictable. It is the most commonly employed and thus perhaps most easily understood by everyone. On the other side of the ledger, some kids—often teenagers—may resent being wrestled away most days from longtime friends if they live with a custodial parent who moves them away from their old neighborhood. Finally, very young children may have special needs in terms of length of visit and care. For example, they may have a tough time leaving their custodial parent for a long period of time.

Full or Sole Custody

As the terms imply, full or sole custody usually involves a situation where one parent has virtually or actual total custody, as well as sole decision-making rights and responsibilities. Often, this occurs if the other parent has had his or her rights terminated, has passed away, or has simply abandoned the children. Full custody requires no agreement or permission from the other biological parent for any parental action, including moving out of the state or country.

Joint Custody

This brand of custody has gained favor within the last decade. Again, individual states may refer to this arrangement as shared custody, shared physical custody, shared primary custody, and/or joint custody. Generally, most forms of joint custody mean that both biological parents are nearly equal in having the children in their respective residences, along with nearly equal rights, responsibilities, and decision making. In most cases, it does not mean that the time spent in residence with each parent is precisely the same. What it does imply is that both parents are deeply involved in caring for their child's needs.

Joint custody does have its disadvantages as well. With more changes from house to house, there is more frequent contact with the ex-spouse. There are timing issues, kids' belongings in the wrong place when needed, and more issues to negotiate; thus, there is greater potential for conflict with the "wicked ex." For obvious reasons, the kids might take on the feeling of being gypsies, too, as opposed to having a home base. Some kids hardly know what to say when asked, "Where do you live?" since they jump back and forth between their mom's and dad's home.

The divorcing parties need to decide on a few important issues—hopefully in advance of the court order—including school selections, medical and other emergency procedures, summer activities, as well as financial issues. Child support, for obvious reasons, takes on quite a different meaning in the joint custody arrangement. Should disputes occur, an experienced mediator can be of great help in arriving at a fair and acceptable decision.

Split Custody

Split custody arrangements occasionally are granted when two or more stepchildren are in the picture. One or more of the children might live with one biological parent, while another may live with the other one. An example might be when a teenage or older son and his father have a very close relationship, so the teen lives with his father—but his sister decides to live with her mother (this is a common arrangement).

The divorcing parents need to take their children's preferences into consideration regarding where they would prefer to live. For obvious reasons, basing custody decisions solely on their preferences can be a disaster. All too often, teenagers prefer to live with the more lenient parent who supervises very little. The stability and character of each parent might be a better factor on which to base such an important choice. We've also seen issues where children feel obligated to take care of parents who have difficulty negotiating life for themselves. They may worry excessively about that parent and/or feel guilty for not being there for them.

Is Adoption Feasible?

Situations often occur that make the adoption of a stepchild by either stepparent feasible or necessary. For example, you might consider it when the child's other biological parent has simply vanished or has passed away. Drs. Emily B. and John S. Visher, founders of the Stepfamily Association of America, make the all-important point that adoption installs certain legal rights and responsibilities and provides a universal family last name, but it does not create or necessarily enhance the new couple's relationship. Further, adoption does not, in and of itself, ensure the bonding, cohesion, or happiness within the adoptive family. The Vishers go on to say, "Your day-to-day interaction, acceptance and enjoyment of each other are what will determine your relationship."

Adoption requires the permission of both biological parents. Often a biological parent who has had scant contact with the child may refuse to grant permission. Children who are asked whether they would like to be adopted by a stepparent are usually conflicted between appearing disloyal to their biological parent and offending their adoptive parent. Seek professional intervention to determine what best meets the needs of the children without putting them in a compromising position. Teens can be given more input into the decision, but it's impossible for very young children to know where their best interests lie when they have such loyalty to both parents regardless of the past.

At any rate, adoption can be complex and involve many people, including not only the child but also the biological parents, adoptive parents, the couple's natural children, as well as extended family members. Again, if you are considering this path, consult with both legal and mental health adoption experts.

We know of situations where stepparents consider adopting children who are in no way related to either individual in the adoptive couple. Such folks seem to just love children and enjoy a larger family—and that's great! Just consider the same issues and suggestions mentioned above.

Long-Distance Stepparenting

There are probably many times when a parent wishes his or her ex-wife or -husband lived on another continent. The "every other weekend" arrangement or other involvement by the noncustodial biological parent can sometimes prove difficult and disruptive in the daily life of a new family trying to come together. But even though a new family has formed, children still have loyalty to their biological mother or father with whom they no longer live. Having a relationship and staying in contact are healthy for the child unless there were extreme circumstances of neglect or abuse.

How does it work, then, when the other biological parent lives in another town or even another state? Terms regarding visitation are usually defined at the time of divorce, but as with everything, needs and circumstances change. Your situation might call for children in your new family to spend extended time in the summer or over the holidays with their other biological parent. "Reentry" back into the family on the return might take some time. You may have stepchildren visiting you under the same circumstances if your husband's children live with their biological mom in another city or state. When you have such limited or interrupted contact, you must work hard to include those children and help them meld into the family. Their unfamiliarity with you, possibly your children, and your lifestyle present you with the challenge of making sure they do feel a part of the family, and not like a guest or a stranger. We have a familiar theme running throughout this book, and that is the needs for security and comfort, whether it is the child *or* the parent. It's important to feel not only *wanted* but also valued and a sense of belonging.

Imagine sending your young child off to visit his or her biological father in another state. It would be extremely difficult for most to put a young child on a train or plane and wave goodbye. You'll need to consider these issues beforehand:

- How is the transportation managed, and who pays for the cost?
- Does Mom or Dad meet the child at the airport, pick them up at your house, or do you just meet at a halfway point?
- Can you figure out a way for children to keep belongings and clothes at both homes to avoid dragging things back and forth?
- Make certain that both parents accept responsibility for homework and school obligations and requirements. It should never fall solely on the shoulders of only the custodial parent.

Consider the fear your children *or* stepchildren may have about leaving "home" for an extended period and making a trip to visit the other parent. This could be a traumatic experience, and it's your responsibility to minimize fears in the best way that you can. Work with the other biological parent, whether your ex or your husband's ex. If you have concerns about the influence the other parent may have on the child, keep in mind that he or she may have the same concerns about you and your home. We have seen circumstances where a child is totally upset at having to leave "home" for a visitation with the other parent, particularly if it involves a far distance and extended period. Whether you are the "sender" or the "receiver" of a child in this situation, be cognizant of the child's emotions and do your best to make the transition as smooth as possible.

Custody of Step-Pets: Dogs, Birds, Cats, Snakes, and More

"But honey, little Sarah loves both her Newfoundlands so much. They sleep with her. And they shouldn't be separated." We told you to meet all extended family members well ahead of time, didn't we? Well, maybe the vet will give you a discount for the two of them. There's no doubt: kids love their pets. So if your stepchildren have one (or five), know that it (they) may need to be welcomed into your new family's home. Often, it's the abrupt nature of acquiring the care and feeding of new mouths that might be disruptive to a new family. Again, knowing what's in store helps you mentally digest the situation and devise coping mechanisms. Like installing hardwood rather than carpeted floors.

Becoming the "Taxi" Stepmom

Merged families—particularly those that include "his," "hers," and perhaps an anticipated "ours," create extra and sometimes elaborate responsibilities. We simply mention at this point that your particular custody arrangement, be it primary, full, joint, or split, will dictate to a degree just what your responsibilities as a stepparent may be. The nature and number of existing and newly created family units is also a factor. Frequently, the new stepmom gets to be the taxi driver, perhaps by default. Since this kind of situation can get really demanding, we do hope that you and your partner have talked about and planned in detail just how you plan to manage this. Suggestions regarding the kids' transportation are detailed in Chapter 10.

Unanticipated Custody and Custody Renegotiation

The adage "The only thing you can count on in life is change" is never so true as in custody situations. Life requires continuous adaptation. Just when you thought you had everything figured out and running smoothly, someone or something throws you a curve. You and your husband get older (and, hopefully, wiser). The kids—especially younger ones—experience eye-popping changes. Remember, in terms of changes, the year between ages two and three is like eons compared to that between ages fourteen and fifteen. Additionally, for whatever reason, you might inherit an unanticipated custody situation because of an unexpected event. When these and other such changes occur, custody arrangements frequently need to be renegotiated. Below are some noteworthy situations requiring renegotiation:

- Geographic moves of one or both parents. Now we have new travel expenses and changes in frequency and duration of visits.
- Changes in schools attended. Before it was Eden Elementary School for six years, now it's Northside Middle School, and the kids' biological mom's house is closer. See where we're going with this?
- Lengthy illness and/or disability of biological mom. This may mean her household is no longer capable of handling current custody arrangements.
- The untimely passing of the biological mom. All of a sudden, you've become a full-time mom to his kids.
- The development of a new interest of a child. And a legendary tennis coach lives across the street—and offers lessons at a legendary price.
- New responsibilities for you, your husband, or the biological mom. An example might be when care is abruptly necessary for an extended family member.

- Irreconcilable differences between a child and any new family member. Despite valiant efforts on everyone's part, a change of environment becomes necessary.

A Case in Point: The Maternal Bond

Lena married a man she thought was her perfect partner. He had custody of his two teenage sons because their mother left them and the family to further her own pursuits. Not only did the biological mother give up custody of her sons, she had little or no contact with them and took no interest in their sports or school activities. Lena's heart was in the right place as she tried to give love and support to the boys, but she didn't presume to hop right into a "mom" role. She involved herself in their lives and activities to let them know she cared and wanted them to have two encouraging parents.

It seems their birth mother wasn't interested in parenting the boys *until* another "mom" entered the scene. All of a sudden, their birth mom reappeared on the scene with a renewed interest and "played the mommy card." Lena had to figure out how to not take this personally and keep in mind what was best for the boys. She tells us, "It was hard to find any compassion for this woman who walked out on her family. I just wanted her to leave us alone. But I had to keep thinking about what was best for the boys, and estrangement from their mom certainly was not. There is a bond there that is very hard to break. I didn't want to be the cause of more conflict, so I had to totally back off. It wasn't easy to refrain from commenting, but I just let the boys make their own decisions regarding their mother without any input or opinions from me. It was equally hard for my husband, who had his own share of resentment." We empathize with Lena in this case and applaud her wise judgment.

REFLECTIONS: KEY ISSUES IN CHAPTER 5

- Custody arrangements come in four basic types. Each has its own sizes and shapes. Know his kids' arrangement as well as parents' rights and responsibilities in your state of residence.

- Identify your new basic family unit and its subunits. Each can have a bearing on the success of your custody arrangement.

- Long-distance stepparenting poses unique challenges. Anticipate and plan for it.

- You might want to consider adoption in one form or another to establish your new family.

- Merging families may "promote" you to the role of "Taxi Mom." Research and plan for this well ahead of time.

- Life changes things, including custody arrangements. Unanticipated events may necessitate custody renegotiations.

Part Two

Day-to-Day Life

Chapter 6

Listening and Relating to His Kids' Biological Mom

Notice that the title of this chapter is not "Avoiding and Hating His Kids' Mother." That's because it's in your best interest to work with her as you create your new family. If you can cooperate with his kids' birth mom, you'll make a powerful ally in your quest for natural and positive relationships with your inherited stepchildren. But how do you do it? First, get to know her on your terms—not by what you've heard. Do not open by talking. Begin by listening. Listening:

- Allows you to assess her rearing practices, values, and hopes for her offspring.
- Tells her that her input is important to you.
- Helps you to gain valuable data about each of her children.
- Builds trust, making communication between the two of you more honest.
- Helps you sense any remaining hurt feelings from what may have been an unwanted change in her lifestyle.

Offering their mom this level of consideration and cooperation means that you two can use teamwork in working toward the same goals you have for the kids. You'll also find that it makes planning and handling visitations, vacations, and holidays so much easier.

How to Approach His Kids' Biological Mom

One of the most difficult challenges you may face as a stepmom is dealing with the mother of your husband's children. There may be a million extenuating circumstances that dictate how you feel about this woman. The particulars of the divorce, with whom the children reside, how much input and influence she has, and how she feels about you are all factors that may influence your relationship. First and foremost, never lose sight of the fact that she is and will remain their mom.

Beyond that, you probably have lots of questions about her. Did she abandon the children for another life? Did she leave their father in anger and take the children away from him, refusing to cooperate with visitation and custody? Is *he* the one that ended the marriage, leaving her with anger and resentment? Trying to understand what the circumstances really were by listening to her may help you to have a better grip on the emotions involved, but should not play a role in how you attempt to relate to her. Remember that you're the newcomer on the scene. Regardless of the particulars, put your feelings aside and strive for the best possible relationship with your stepchildren's mom. She's probably going to be a continual part of your lives, like it or not. The children need her, and in spite of all of the possible adult screwups, they will usually be fiercely loyal to their mom.

Give Her a Chance to Get Comfortable with You

By developing a relationship slowly, you allow her to "break the ice" and vent if she needs to. Perhaps she wants to share her side of the story or her feelings on the changes her ex-husband and children are facing. You will also let her know that you're not a threat to her role as "mom." Many women feel very threatened by another woman with "mom" as a part of her moniker. The very last thing you want to do is pose a threat to the biological mom by overriding her decisions (unless they pose a danger to the children) or undermining her authority as a parent.

Keep Negative Thoughts to Yourself!

If you dislike her, and we will stress this repeatedly, do *not* display those feelings in front of her or the children. It will be self-defeating. Instead, let her know that you are not here to take her place as parent or in any way discredit her. Make every attempt to be courteous and respectful. Tell her that you are open to any discussion regarding the children and their well-being. If she sees that you truly have the best interests of her children at heart, she may well feel less threatened and try to treat you with mutual respect.

The circumstances of your custody arrangements may have great bearing on the way you feel. If the children live with you and you are the one who takes care of them while their biological mom breezes in and out at her convenience, it will be very difficult to continue being nice to her. Yet even in the most trying circumstances like these, remain civil and respectful. You'll probably have to bury your feelings and bite your tongue, but it will benefit everyone in the long run, and you'll be glad you did.

If you truly do care about the welfare of your stepchildren, you will *never* malign their mom in any way. This includes sarcasm, eye-rolling, or any derogatory expressions. Resist the urge to align yourself with your teenaged stepchildren when they vent about their mom. Trust us: the kids will remember *any* negative expression from you and will bring it up at the worst possible moment. You can be a good listener without participating in any negativity. You may think to yourself, "Aha! They finally see their mother for the witch she is." Don't say it. Listen if they need you to, but refrain from commenting. You'll be pretty good at biting your tongue by the time your stepkids are grown. (It will all be worth it.)

Tell Her That You Respect Her Input

Whether you and your husband have full custody or not, it's important to let the kids' birth mother know that you value her opinions and input. Ask her for ideas and suggestions about things that affect the children. The information she gives you will help you establish a better relationship with your stepkids, as well as their mom. Be up front and direct. Never put your husband in the middle or make him the messenger. If you approach the children's mom with respect and without a confrontational attitude, your relationship may get off to a good start and even get better with time. If she will have nothing to do with you, your hands may be tied for now, but don't give up. Again, if she doesn't see you as a threat, your efforts at communication may eventually be rewarded.

Commend Her for Aspects of Good Parenting

Every parent is pleased to hear compliments extended about his or her children. Try to tell the mom directly that the positives of her parenting make you appreciate your time with her children. Compliment her for specifics of their behavior and attitude. If you think her parenting includes more negatives than positives, keep those thoughts to yourself. Keep in mind that whatever problems you may have with the children may not necessarily be her fault. Most parents really do have the best interests of their children in mind and do the best job that they are capable of doing. Search for the good. Bear in mind that the mom herself may not have experienced the best parenting in the world. She loves her children, but may simply have never learned good parenting skills.

Ask for Valuable Data about Each Child's Nature

In most circumstances, nobody knows a child better than the mother. She's probably the one who has done most of the nurturing and caring for her children since birth. The bond between a mother and child is very deep and usually unbreakable. You never want to drive a wedge into that relationship. Instead, try to get as much helpful information as you can about each child that will make your job as a stepmom easier. (See page 94 in this chapter for more specific information on what to ask.)

Again, how you approach her is crucial. You're not trying to pump her for information, but you are trying to find out more about the children's personalities, routines, and even quirks. She likely will appreciate your concern when you ask her for suggestions about what you can do to make their time with you happy and beneficial; if so, she will tell you what you want to know.

Accept whatever she tells you with grace and gratitude. If you think some of her suggestions are not helpful or even ridiculous, thank her just the same. Certainly, we're not telling you to let her dictate what your relationship with your stepchildren should be. The point is to take as much information as you can in order to do what's best for the kids.

Assure Her That You Care about Her Children

Of course, parents are incredibly sensitive about how people treat and relate to their children. Most biological moms feel an unsettling insecurity when someone else begins sharing the "mom" role with their children. No matter how lightly you tread, it's difficult to assure someone that you care deeply about her children's welfare, yet you're not trying to take over and be their mom. Kathleen told us that she assured her stepchildren in the beginning that she was *not* trying to be their mom or take their mom's place in any way. Having that statement out in the open let the kids know her place in their life.

Circumstances dictate how much of a mom you need to be. Do the children live with you, or do you have them every other weekend? Regardless of how limited or extensive your time with the children may be, you must assure their biological mom that your concern for the children is sincere and well intentioned. She needs to know that you and your husband are respectful in your comments about her in front of the children.

Keep Disagreements Between the Two of You

Unfortunately, even with your best effort, you may find yourself in a disagreement with the kids' mom. Regardless of circumstances, who says what to whom, and who gets the last word, you must put the welfare of the children first. Their emotional health and security are dependent upon how the adults in their lives conduct themselves. You are the ones who direct the environment and set the stage, so be adults. If you need to work out an issue, do so away from the children and in a calm manner.

Establish Open and Honest Communication

The majority of this chapter deals with the importance of being open, honest, and respectful in communicating with the children's biological mother. We know there are times when the birth mother will refuse to have any communication with you whatsoever. See what you can do to change that. But don't use your husband, and *certainly* not the children, as carrier pigeons. When someone else is the messenger, you run the risk of misinformation being delivered. If you aren't comfortable meeting with her face to face, consider other methods of communication (which we'll talk about shortly).

Gauge Leftover Animosities but Stay Out of Them

Your husband and his ex-wife may have a lengthy history about which you are unaware or only know part of. Of course, you know all of the things he has told you, and you need to be unconditionally supportive of your spouse. However, you'll also have contact with his ex-wife on a continual basis. Continue to be supportive of your spouse, but form your own opinions while establishing a working relationship with his ex. There are always two sides to every story, so resist the temptation to assign blame. Remove yourself from conflict and controversy. Try to be a neutral party who is just trying to watch out for the children's best interests.

You also have no idea what opinion his ex-wife may have formed about you and what she thinks is on your agenda. Were you in any way a part of your husband's decision to divorce his previous wife? If so, she may be angry about what happened and take it out on you. Still, harboring resentment and animosity is counterproductive, especially when it comes to the children. If you continually remind her that they're what's most important, she may put aside her pain and try to create a relationship of civility and respect.

A common fear we heard from new stepmoms was that you don't know what she really thinks of you, and what she has said about you to her children. How do her feelings affect the children and their relationship with you? There's not much you can do about this except carry yourself with dignity and don't give her anything to complain about. And, as always, keep the best interest of the kids at heart.

We know that no matter how secure a person you are in your own right, you always know that he chose her first, even if he didn't know you when they got married. Get past that. You really have no idea what circumstances were in place, and people do change. Move on.

The relationship between you and the kids' mom will play a critical role in what kind of adults the children will become. Always keep in mind your long-range goals for the children. Try to remember this isn't about you, but directly or indirectly your behavior and acceptance will go a long way in bringing about positive interaction.

Talk to Her about the Kids

When you're at a point in your relationship that you feel comfortable asking your husband's ex about her kids, you'll still need to proceed with caution. Try to have this conversation in person or on the phone—avoid e-mail unless there's no other way. Obviously, you want to catch her in a good mood before plunging into a list of questions regarding her children. Start with the most benign issues. Understand that she may still be experiencing negative feelings regarding unwanted life changes. Or she may be relieved that the divorce is final. This is why you take her emotional temperature as a first step—it could vary widely.

When the time is right, try asking her some of these questions:

- "What do they like and not like to do?"
- "What do they like and not like to eat?"
- "What special abilities, interests, and needs does each child have?"
- "How is each child best motivated? What turns each one off?"
- "Are they always truthful?" (Listen well here.)
- "Are there issues about which they feel badly (or guilty)?"
- "Should I be checking whether each follows through on things?"
- "Are there other issues I should be watching for?"
- "What are each child's hopes and dreams?"

Treat the above issues as casual interest only; don't make it a psychological interrogation. Choose language that is comfortable for you.

Show Sincere Interest

Sooner or later, in one way or another, his kids will probably find out that you were asking their mom about them. Don't worry about it. Your sincere interest shows them that you care. If the kids are angry that you learned whatever you learned, think about why that might be. Maybe you found out something embarrassing about them? A personality trait they're not proud of? Whatever it is, know that their initial anger will subside, and they will appreciate that you cared enough to ask.

Remember that all of us like to be accepted as we are—for our positives and perceived negatives. Knowing that you know their biggest blunders and screwups—and still care is abundantly comforting and healing for them. It goes without saying that you keep the information in confidence and use it appropriately. This can be a solid building block to your bonding process.

Engage in Cooperation, Not Competition

Cooperation is working as a team in pursuing a common goal. The best athletic teams result from a well-thought-out plan; consistent practice; and everyone supporting, defending, and protecting each other. Winning teams do not always have the best overall talent, but they are always the most cohesive in that all individuals have come to trust, rely upon, and sense every move of their teammates. Naturally, this requires an in-depth knowledge of the others' special skills, methods, inclinations, and goals. How do teammates get this knowledge? Through reflective listening, positively phrased questions, and effective use of the various modes of communication.

Obviously, it takes time, energy, and skill to develop an attitude of teamwork when everyone initially might be running in different directions. Yes, there will be mistakes, misunderstandings, and backslidings, but with dedicated effort, improvement should occur over time. Learn to spot and reinforce the smallest evidences of improvement.

Competition implies winning, conquering, and outclassing another. This may be okay for individual and team sports, but it is never okay when the object is the healthy development of another human being. Your relationship with the kids' biological mom might begin with a sense of competition and negative feelings; that's normal. However, with dedicated goals and a bit of artfulness on your part, initial competition should turn to cooperation and mutual respect over time. We've heard many biological moms who applaud the stepmom's relationship and efforts with their children. We promise, we really have heard statements like, "I couldn't have asked for a better stepmom for my kids." This is the result of cooperation, not competition.

Structuring Visitations, Vacations, and Holidays

The topic of holidays and vacations is so intense that we have devoted most of Chapter 11 to it. Still, it's worth mentioning that the effort you put into having a good relationship with the children's mom will pay off when you try to arrange these events. Though you may think it would break your heart not to have the whole family together for a special event, respect the fact that she probably feels the same way. It's just a fact of life that your holidays and vacations will not always be the way you would like when you are living in a blended family. Also, don't take it personally if your stepkids want to be with their mom on Christmas morning. New situations are difficult to understand at times and take adjustment. Kids generally like things to stay the same, so be patient and do your best to make sure you are sensitive to what they may be feeling. Your feelings and needs are important, and we are not discrediting them; however, some of this just goes with the territory in being part of a blended family.

Establish Modes of Communication

With biological moms, as with anyone, having a variety of communication modes is an advantage to you. Let's review some of the basic communication modes and their unique characteristics:

- **Verbal.** Face to face and phone. Face-to-face verbal contact is the broadest and most inclusive category. It includes eye contact, good listening (yes, there's that word again), your choice of words, pacing, pauses, inflections, questioning, clarification, intonation, loudness of voice, and emphasizing selected words. Quite a list, right? Face-to-face contact also makes available the all-important nonverbal modes discussed below. Phone communication is probably the most widely used, because of its convenience, but it is less personal, particularly when voice mail and text messaging are used. In certain situations, many of us may prefer the greater anonymity of phone and voice mail contact, but usually it's when we have axes to grind or want to say "No." If this is the case with you and the kids' birth mom, keep working on building trust and establishing open and honest communication and it should become less and less necessary over time.
- **Nonverbal.** Nonverbal modes of communication are very telling. They include facial expressions, posture, positioning, body movements, eye contact, and even the physical distance between the communicators. Some folks literally invade another's personal space and get in their face. Others distance themselves safely from those with whom they converse. In truth, we are often unaware of many of our own bodily communications. Check yours out. Ask a friend for feedback. Or have a videotape made of you interacting with another person. Having done so, you may be quite pleased with many of your antics, while others might make you wince.
  Nonverbal messages are usually more credible than verbal ones, most likely because we are less conscious of them and

thus do not attempt to disguise them. Note also that words said to one person might communicate praise while to another the exact same words may be a putdown. How the statement is meant depends on the prior relationship with the individual as well as intonation, facial features, posture, and so on. Getting to know your own verbal and nonverbal habits and styles helps you to become more authentic and to know others' meaning more thoroughly.

- **Written communication.** Written communication comes in the form of letters, e-mails, and notes, as well as text messages. What's being written varies widely—praise, appreciation, directions, requests, suggestions, lists, and so on. Written communication has the capability of being more detailed and comprehensive than the verbal type because it provides a record and is capable of being mass-produced. In terms of your relationship with the kids' mom, consider sending her a note of praise, encouragement, affection, or appreciation. Such notes say, "I understand, appreciate, and applaud what you are doing with your kids." What mom would not be grateful for that? Written communications can be powerful bond builders.

- **Communicating in groups.** Groups in which both biological moms and stepmoms are present range from being fairly formal (such as graduations, weddings, birthdays, and more) to casual residential gatherings and carry-ins. In some cases, you may see the biological mom (and her significant other, if she has one) at virtually every party you attend. For the most part, this is healthy as long as everyone is content, free of animosity, and even enjoys getting together. Impossible, you say? Not really. It happens all the time. And whenever both biological mom and stepmom are present at the same event, with or without their respective new life partners, cordiality, courtesy, and respect should continue to be the standards of the day.

If the Kids' Mom Remarries

Perhaps the children's mother found a new love and is moving on with her personal life. Or perhaps she found someone to help her get back at her ex. If your husband's divorce was ugly and filled with resentment, he and his ex-wife probably still share a lot of hostility. If he gets married to you before she remarries, she may try to even the score by remarrying as well. If she finds a nice guy and makes a good decision in so doing, at least she's keeping the kids' best interest in mind. If, however, she settled for someone whose presence is not healthy for the kids, she's put the children in the middle of this score-settling battle with her husband. This is, of course, one of the worst things that parents can do to a child.

The Changes in Store

If the kids' biological mom remarries, under whatever circumstances, they now have another person invested in their lives and welfare. This can obviously be a good thing if her new partner is a wonderfully supportive person who helps everyone keep things in perspective and has only the best interests of the children in mind. But he may be the type to want to step in and take control and make decisions that are not in tune with the ones you have made.

You, as with all things, need to work together with your partner and try to communicate effectively with this new stepdad. He will have lots of influence, especially if the children are living with him. Recognize that you can't control another person and what goes on in his home. If his opposition to you and your decisions causes major conflict, now is the time to be rational and cooperative and seek outside intervention. Just make sure that you *never put the children in a compromising position.*

Her remarriage may also mean a potential custody change. She may desire more, or possibly less, time with the children. Chapter 5 discusses custody issues at length. Renegotiation is always a possibility, even though it is far better to reach agreement without the help of the courts. There are all kinds of options and all kinds of arrangements that can be worked out; keep the kids' interests at heart when making these kinds of changes.

Act Like Adults

The bottom line is that all parties must remember to act in the best interests of the children. Put your insecurities aside and be the adults. Sit down together and agree on how things can be done. If you can't agree, engage a mediator; or, as a last resort, let the courts decide.

A life lesson: Learn to live with and accept that which you cannot control. The one thing you *can* always control is your own behavior. Do whatever it takes to make the kids feel secure about their new stepdad and let them know your love and support will always be there. Don't ever take any satisfaction in hearing the children say they don't like their new stepdad, as it makes the time spent there worrisome and unpleasant for all of you. Listen to them, but try to be positive. Be in tune with their reasons, however, as you need to protect your children and stepchildren from possible harm or mistreatment. Yes, it is very difficult to have someone outside your immediate family making decisions that you do not agree with about the children. Still, keep your anger checked and do not display it in front of the kids.

If the underlying issue is your husband's unresolved baggage with his ex, don't make it worse by adding your two cents against her. In addition, leave the kids out of it. They have been torn apart enough by the divorce itself. Never put them in a situation where they must divide loyalties.

It Can Work

We actually have seen situations where both sets of parents communicate well and get along with each other. The pressure on the kids is therefore minimized, and everyone's life is so much less stressful. As the children get older, you might find acceptance becomes easier. You have graduations, weddings, and grandchildren in the future. These can be pleasant experiences where all involved can find joy, or they can be competitive, nightmarish experiences. How you handle yourself at these events is the key. It might not be easy, but do what is best for the happiness of the children that you helped raise.

A Case in Point: Changes in Attitude

Iris and her new husband have full custody of his two teen-aged children (who see their birth mom one weekend a month) and her ten-year-old daughter from a previous marriage. The boys' birth mother calls them constantly, driving Iris crazy. Iris felt that this interfered with their own family life and the spirit they were trying to establish. She preferred that their mom call them at designated times when calling "just to chat," and not (as she often did) during mealtimes. Iris felt that she did everything humanly possible to have a respectful and civil relationship with her husband's ex-wife. Her personal opinion of their biological mom was quite low, as she perceived her to have abandoned her kids to go off and have her own life. She didn't want the responsibility of her two teenagers but certainly resented anyone else trying to take her place in the role of mom, according to Iris. Yet, she is their mom, and no demographics will ever change that.

Here is a situation with a biological mom seeing her children being parented by another woman and desperately trying to reclaim her position. The biological mom felt threatened by everything Iris did. She therefore wanted to begin playing a more active role in their lives, which in turn frustrated Iris and caused her to question what her own responsibilities were. "I was the one with all of the work and responsibility. I'm the one who drove them to practice, the mall, wherever they needed to go. I took care of our house, picked up after them, invited their friends over, and did the cooking—all of the grunt work. When it came time for any recognition at school or church, their biological mom waltzed in and took all of the credit. It made me crazy."

A year or two after Iris remarried, so did her ex-husband. Although Iris tried to be cordial to her daughter's new stepmom, she felt herself resenting the other woman's role in her child's life. She, too, didn't like another person involved in any decision making or in having influence over *her* daughter. After all, the latter was only ten, and what right did her ex-husband's wife have to play a parenting role when the child only visited and didn't live there?

It wasn't until Iris stepped back and really examined her own frustration and emotions that she could consider how the mother of her stepchildren must feel. Iris considered herself a secure and well-grounded person, yet she felt that security waver when someone else was in the mom role, even if only for short periods. "I finally realized that even though the kids' mom wouldn't, or couldn't, handle the responsibility of teenagers, she must love them as desperately as I do my child. I stepped back and stopped trying to assert myself in the mom role as forcefully as I had been. In truth, I learned to relax when it came to their birth mom. I even encouraged more contact with her. Eventually, because of better communication, the tension seemed to ease between us. That attitude change on my part seemed to extend toward my daughter's stepmom as well."

Although Iris's feelings toward her own daughter's stepmom are still a work in progress, she has stopped feeling so threatened and trusts the bond she has with her daughter.

None of us can ever really get inside the head of another person to know who she is or why she makes the choices she does. Iris saw her stepkids' mom only as someone who abandoned her children. People don't have their children with them for any number of reasons. As we have said repeatedly, most people love their children unconditionally and do the best they can under the circumstances. Unless the children were abused or neglected, give their birth mom the benefit of the doubt. Generosity of heart and spirit will never cease to work for the advantage of all involved. Getting her to trust you, your judgment regarding the kids' daily needs and lives, and your genuine concern for the children will lay the foundation for a positive relationship between the two of you. Chances are she's not going anywhere, and hopefully neither are you.

REFLECTIONS: KEY ISSUES IN CHAPTER 6

- Open first conversations with the birth mom by listening, careful questioning, and assessing.

- Listening usually says more than talking.

- Listening tells her you value her input. It gives her a chance to get comfortable with you and vent a bit. It assures her that you truly care about her children. It builds trust, cooperation, and honest communication, and it allows you to assess her current emotions and goals for her children.

- Kids will know—and appreciate (even if not immediately)—that you've asked caring questions.

- A cooperative relationship means that the two of you are working together toward common goals.

- Cooperation makes the planning and handling of visitations, vacations, and holidays much easier for all.

- Skill in a variety of communication modes benefits everyone. Review the special uses and advantages of verbal, nonverbal, written, and group communication.

- Should the birth mom remarry, anticipate changes in her emotions and behavior for a time.

Chapter 7

Sharing Daddy with His Kids

"His kids love their dad. He's been their rock. He always had his special time with them. I know I won't feel envious when he's alone with them shopping and at out-of-town ballgames. After all, he and I had lots of time together when we were dating. But I can give that up. There will be those great times, too, when all of us are together. I know he'll be a great model for my kids as well."

They were a unit before—Daddy and his kids—before the big divorce. And they should continue to be. If you play this one wisely, you can all have what you had before and more. There is something special about the interaction and bond kids have with this man called Daddy.

Your Partner with His Kids

Kids in a group are a microcosm of how they might relate to future groups and gatherings. Group dynamics can be fascinating to observe. You see all sorts of personality factors and emotional responses emerge, including assertiveness or timidity, egocentrism or sensitivity, quickness to understand and longer learning curves, team players and individualists, the outspoken and the reserved—in short, a menagerie of traits ranging from one end of the continuum to the other. Groups provide a forum in which to spot differences and special interests that need reinforcement and nurture. His kids and their Daddy need these special times together. Your facilitation and understanding will be enduringly appreciated.

Each of us is a separate and discreet entity as well as a member of a given group. Kids long for that special individual attention to their unique concerns. It doesn't matter much just what Dad and his kids do in these precious periods. It is that they are together in the moment. Kids know when a parent is one with them in action and thought. *This is the stuff of which bonding is made.* Put aside any feelings of jealousy you may have and encourage him to spend time with his children.

Your Partner with Your Kids

The same benefits accrue when Dad is with your kids as well. Actually, his attention to them is a special bonus. He doesn't have to care, but he does. Since everyone is different, most stepparents will have certain skills and interests that the biological parents do not. What better mentoring and modeling can you get? It's like having private lessons, but this teacher has a deeper, more personal, and longer-term investment. Skills children learn from stepdad (or stepmom) can serve as creative outlets or necessary skills that they can use recreationally or vocationally for the rest of their lives. Children thus become broadened in a way they would not otherwise have been and can give and share more with their own children one day. A stepparent's legacy, like any parent's, therefore grows exponentially, and his or her link to the future is forged.

Your Partner with His and Your Grandkids

Grandparents can provide so much. If your new husband is a loving grandpa or stepgrandpa, appreciate the precious time he can provide as an interested adult, sage advisor, model of integrity, teacher, and more. One grandfather we know taught his grandson the simple but lost art of whittling—a skill that will serve as a creative outlet for the rest of his life.

Your Partner with Everybody Together

Having everyone together at the same residence or outing can be uniquely rewarding. Preparation is paramount, however, as the lack of structure, guidelines, and boundaries creates chaos. Plan a get-together for all the various family subunits, including Dad, you, his kids, your kids, grandchildren, stepgrandchildren, grandparents, and stepgrandparents. The sheer number of individuals and subgroups in this scenario can be remarkable.

Organize age-appropriate activities to break the ice and enable people to get to know each other while playing games, using recreational equipment, preparing food, and enjoying other entertainments. Be sure you think about logistics such as whether you'll be indoors and/or outdoors, adequate bathrooms, and comfortable seating.

When Daddy and the Kids Are Away

Let's say Daddy has taken his twins on Friday morning to an out-of-state regional soccer tournament. If they win, they will stay another day and play again on Saturday. Should they win on Saturday, they will play in the championship game on Sunday. You could approach this situation in two quite different ways:

1. You could incubate negative feelings of resentment for his kids' taking him away from you—especially after you've gone above and beyond the call of duty in cooking their special dishes, cleaning their messes, taxiing them around, watching their school pageant . . .
2. You can enjoy the respite and do some of those things you've always wanted to do but didn't have time for—like join your girlfriends from your single life for a fun get-together.

We suggest that you hope they do come home with that championship trophy. The weekend also might be an ideal time for you to spend some special time with your own kids. Besides, resentment is too heavy to carry around. Send it packing and focus your thoughts forward to *when you get him for yourself.*

How about His Job?

Some men are better than others about the limits they place on bringing their job issues home. Obviously, some of this is okay. You want to know what he does and how he does it. You want to be a supportive sounding board when needed. (He should reciprocate with you in this way as well, of course.) But he can't spend night after night and hour after hour complaining about work. Set time limits if you have to—say ten or fifteen minutes per evening for him to vent about these issues. Go by the rules. Call "Time" after the agreed-upon interval and divert his thoughts to pleasant events or necessary items needing attention. Don't forget to encourage him when he complies—like with a smile and big hug. (Hint: This is how new behavior is shaped and stamped in. He may not even know what's happened.)

Our jobs are a part of our self-image, to be sure, but only a part. Think of the money you two earn as a means of providing more options in life, not as an end in itself. Men who meet the criteria for workaholics often rationalize, "I'm doing this for you and the kids—so they'll have something later." We don't buy this reasoning. You and the kids need quality time *now*.

Your Partner's Time with His Friends and Relatives

Whether it's poker night with the guys, golfing on Saturday with the boss, or fishing with his brother, some male bonding is healthy for both new and long-term husbands. Excess is the problem. Poker and drinking at the club five nights a week, and golfing or fishing all weekend most weekends is over the line. Guess who gets to mind the children and mop the mansion? That just might be you.

As early as you can in your relationship, talk generally about how you'll both spend free time. Remember, if his past history is full of excesses of this type, these behaviors are likely to continue and be difficult to change. The story comes to mind of a woman who rescued an injured snake and brought him back to health. Upon his recovery, the snake promptly bit his kindly caretaker. "Why on earth did you bite me?" asked the woman. "Well," the reptile replied, "you knew I was a snake!"

A limit of one poker night and a couple of Saturday golfing sessions each month seems reasonable under ordinary circumstances. He, of course, should reciprocate and entertain the kids while you have equivalent time doing whatever you want to do.

Your Partner's Time Spent on His Hobbies

Let us define hobbies here as primarily solitary activities, whereas golf, poker, and tennis, as cited above, occur in social circumstances. Some male hobbies might include woodworking, mechanics, painting, reading, or writing. Some men prefer to fish alone as well. We know of one wife who complained that her mate spent countless hours building a beautiful chest of drawers for her. Yes, it was a lovely gesture, but she would have much preferred to be involved in an activity with him. Another wife urged her husband to find a hobby. He subsequently became obsessively involved in rejuvenating an old classic car and spent less and less time with her. So be careful what you wish for!

Yes, these examples are extreme. But it's not unusual for a man to get a kick from his hobby. The trick for you lies in discovering something that both of you and/or the whole family can experience together. Coming up with these kinds of activities is the ultimate in being creative. Tina, whose husband loved to spend his weekends fishing, nicely solved her problem by getting her own tackle box and fishing rod. She now accompanies her husband and with the kids on weekend fishing trips and even enters bass fishing competitions. Her trophy case has approached the size of his.

"Hey, When Do I Get Him?"

You get him after the soccer tournament and perhaps his golf or fishing outing. Your kids will be with their biological dad and his kids will be with their birth mom. Or you might facilitate their sleeping over with friends whose parents you've met and trust. Just make sure the kids have both his and your cell phone and landline numbers. Tell the kids to check in by phone with Dad and/or you at least once. Communication is the key! Lots of research reveals that kids whose parents demonstrate caring in this way get into significantly less trouble.

Now, after the kids are taken care of, it's just you and Dad—*your new husband*. Your planning will pay dividends.

Your Alone Time with His Kids

This chapter is primarily devoted to sharing your new husband with all children involved, his parents, his job, friends, hobbies, and so on. But we would be remiss if we did not point out that you as a stepmom can provide the same benefits to his children while giving time to your friends and family members as well. Recognize and acknowledge your tremendous power here in teaching useful skills and, even more important, in modeling such values as good character, honesty, and integrity.

A Case in Point: Matt's Stepdad Legacy

Marcy shared the poignant story of her second, but now deceased, husband, Matt, who had been central to the lives of her two daughters. Matt encouraged his younger stepdaughter Andrea's interest in scuba diving and horsemanship, in which he himself was skilled and certified. Subsequently, Andrea became very skilled in scuba diving and is a fine equestrian as well. Andrea's own three daughters have become interested in swimming and riding arts.

Matt also noticed his older stepdaughter Amy's natural inclination toward business management. He got her involved in several of his business enterprises. Currently, Amy is part owner of a large wholesale corporation. Amy's own daughter, Niki, has recently voiced an interest in studying economics at the collegiate level. Thus, Matt's legacy of good stepparenting continues to manifest itself in extended positive links to the future.

REFLECTIONS: KEY ISSUES IN CHAPTER 7

- Facilitate (don't compete with) Daddy's time with his kids and grandkids.

- Your new husband can be a terrific ally in enhancing your own kids' development.

- Stepmoms can be special to all the kids and grandkids involved.

- Enjoy well-planned complete family and stepfamily gatherings.

- Cherish and take advantage of the times when Daddy is away with his kids.

- Plan for and use well those precious times when you and your husband can be alone.

- Good stepparenting provides positive and extended links to the future.

Chapter 8

Creating Family Rituals
of Your Own

Have you and your partner established a schedule regarding when to get up, mealtimes, homework, and bedtimes? Have you created rules for visiting friends, having friends over, and related communication? Have you established curfews? Are the kids accustomed to different rules in their biological mom's house? Isn't this your house? What about etiquette and courtesies? What permissions are necessary? What happens during weekends? Lingering cloudy issues lurk here, say veteran stepmoms.

Suddenly, life gets more complex. You'd come to appreciate the peace, privacy, and independence of having that neat apartment, condo, or cute little house all to yourself. You made it yours in selecting your own favorite colors, carpet, flooring, and furniture. The closets and garage were all yours. But something (actually *someone*) was missing. You've found him. He met almost all the things on your shopping list. Moving in just with him (or he with you) and sharing space, time, and preferences was quite an adjustment in itself. And now his kids will be coming. Whether it's every other weekend or most of time, there will be lots of new family rituals, compromises, and strategies to work out.

When to Get Out of Bed

When joining a new family together, take some time to determine everyone's personal habits, practices, and needs. Don't expect to move in with a schedule posted on the refrigerator for everyone to consult and adhere to. Before you can see how your new family hums along together, try figuring out just where to start. In spite of your possible need for organization and cohesive management, observe long enough to figure out how this new group operates. If the kids have lived with your new husband, they probably already have some kind of system in place. Maybe it's not to your exact specifications and appears a little haphazard, but it's probably worked for them in the past. If your new step-kids are teenagers, we'd say they usually have figured out when to get up, eat, and somehow get to school, work, or practice. If not, you've got some work ahead of you.

Work Together to Establish Routine

Communication before your marriage, or as early as possible, is crucial in determining how your new family will operate. Daily rituals can be as important as the seemingly bigger challenges of holidays and birthdays. After all, you don't want to spend the first week hanging outside the bathroom door waiting for your turn. If you walk in and trip over wet towels and find the hot water depleted, you will start each day angry and frustrated.

We can't stress enough the need for patience. Step back at first and tread slowly. If you come on like a dictator, as in "I'm the adult . . . it's my house!" you will be met with resistance and hostility. Respect and consideration are critical, and kids (his *and* yours) learn best by the example you set. We are not telling you that you don't have needs and demands as well. Just be patient and try to learn as much as you can during the early adjustment period. Letting the kids know when *you* have to be at work or when or if you will be fixing a morning meal will give them a heads-up as to how to participate in a productive morning routine. Again, let them know you are respectful of their needs and are there to help. A schedule that works for all of you will evolve when you and your husband work together and communicate in a caring and loving way.

Mandating that a teenager get up by 9 A.M. on a Saturday morning to mow the grass is an example of how *not* to do it. We're not saying *you* should mow the lawn, but if noon works for him, the grass doesn't mind and will still look nice when he's done. Flexibility, Mom.

Mealtime Etiquette and Expectations

"I like the way my mom fixes it better!"

If you're a person who loves your kitchen and the opportunity to cook for people, having a new family will give you lots of chances to show your stuff. It's fun to cook for a family of hungry people, right? Well . . . maybe not. Those commercials on television where kids applaud their mom for fixing the foods they like are all too often more fantasy than fact. A million different scenarios can occur in the new kitchen:

- The kids are polite and respectful and appreciate the fact that someone is cooking for them at all. (Good luck if you think this will happen right away.)

- They hate everything you fix and refuse to eat it.
- You slave over dinner each night and the kids don't show up because they're doing their own thing with their friends. (Of course, no one told you this.)
- You hate to cook but force yourself so you can be a "good" mom.
- You hate to cook, and so you order out or eat out every night.
- The kids complain about what you fix, so your husband gives them money to order pizza or go out for fast food.

We can't think of anything more frustrating than the last example, but believe us, it happens. Yes, it's very disrespectful to you, but your husband may not know the best approach to take with them. You may hear about how much better "my mom" cooks, but there are better responses than getting angry. You and your husband can and should discuss the ritual of mealtime and food as early as possible. It's a crucial issue that needs to be addressed. So many times, people just expect that those things will "work themselves out," or you'll face it as you go. You can approach it that way if you want, but expect a bumpy road. You'll save yourselves a lot of discord if you at least broach the subject in the beginning.

Respect—and Honor—the Existing Tradition

Obviously, you need to ascertain how meals were handled before you came on the scene. Plus, allowing everyone to have input facilitates harmony and cooperation. You can easily find out what kind of food your stepchildren like and will eat simply by *asking them*. Be sure to ask them how they like each prepared. Let them know that you will try to fix things that way, but it may take some experimenting on your part. A statement such as: "I may not get it exactly like you like it right away, but I'll be trying" or "You just have to give me some feedback," transmits your sincerity. It also lets them know that you want mealtime to be a pleasant experience together. The message to them is that you care about their preferences. Again, you have allowed them to have input, which usually results in less complaining and more appreciation. It may just invite an offer like, "Let me show you." Few bonding opportunities are better than working together on tasks both individuals enjoy. We are by no means saying the children should be in charge of directing and overseeing the food buying and preparation. We are not advocating that you take this to the extreme, but rather that you allow their preferences to be considered as you would in any family.

Be Flexible and Patient

Back in the 1950s, people ate dinner together as an evening ritual. It was when you talked about your day and exchanged ideas. We now live in an era where everyone has different schedules and different timetables. Soccer practice, Scouts, after-school jobs, drama rehearsal, and gymnastics lessons have to be scheduled and accounted for. If there is *any* way you can sit down together as a family in the evenings, we highly recommend it, as there is nothing like sitting across the table from someone and sharing food to foster open and honest communication.

Despite your best efforts, however, not everyone will be present at every meal, and not everyone will be pleased with the food you prepare. Don't take it personally when the kids say they don't like something. Your own children probably do the same thing. In practical terms, simply do your best to have food available in the evenings so everyone can eat by their own timetable. That may be your best option. It's not ideal, but you have to work within the confines of everyone's frenzied schedules in today's world.

Finally, you and your husband can determine what your expectations should be regarding etiquette and table manners. Even better, solicit the kids' ideas on table etiquette as well. Base your expectations on your family dynamics and individual differences and needs. We know this could be either no big deal or a huge task and challenge in your family. There can be a lot of emotion wrapped around food and eating habits, including even disorders. Make sure that your contribution lends itself to healthy living and healthy relationships rather than excessive formality.

Homework

Unless the words "Go do your homework" mean you might have a little peace and quiet, most parents as well as their children dread that phrase. Doing homework back in the day meant working studiously at the kitchen table or in the child's bedroom—a scenario straight out of *Leave It to Beaver*. Today, with practice, meetings, two working parents, fast food, video games, iPods, cell phones, dinner, television, and the computer, getting to homework can present a huge challenge. Let's face it, they've been in school all day, and you have been at work. Sitting down for an evening of homework can seem pretty unappealing. Kids are likely to put it off until the last possible minute and, of course, not before 9 P.M. Sunday night.

Help Them Help Themselves

Kids can rope you into taking over their homework with the simple plea, "I need help." Of course, you have to be supportive; you have to lend a hand when they need it, especially if you have a child who struggles academically. Be sure to communicate and discuss homework strategies with your husband so you two are on the same page. If he is better with one subject than you are, then he can pitch in too. If you have a better handle on math, then you need to be the helper.

Set aside a time for homework and a quiet place. Granted, your fast-paced schedules may not allow total consistency, but at least you've made the effort. If your stepkids are at your house on schoolnights, like it or not, you have to make the effort with a homework regimen and assistance if and where needed.

Talk with your child's teacher and get suggestions on what the child's academic needs and progress may be. The school and teacher are your best partners in cooperative efforts for success.

Kids Hanging Out with Friends

What's the first thing kids ask when you are planning a family dinner at a restaurant or some other outing? That's right. "Can I bring a friend?" Of course, you want your children to be happy and hang with the right kind of people starting at an early age. And you don't want your child to be a loner, but nor do you want to let them compromise values for so-called popularity. It's a tough balance.

At any age, you have to set certain standards for behavior in your home. Your kids should know what kind of language is allowed, TV rituals, raiding the kitchen, using the CD and DVD player, and the computer and Internet. You also want your home to be open and welcoming (within reason), and for the kids and their friends to feel comfortable there. You can be vigilant without hovering. Know what they're doing and what they're watching. You are responsible for what goes on in your home, and that includes other people's children.

Young Children

You will likely find that you encounter fewer difficulties with young children who want to play with friends. You'll probably organize which friends they see, when, and for how long. Keep in mind that you have lots of influence about whom they socialize with when they're young, but once they move up in the grade levels, parental wisdom becomes less important to them.

Preteens and Teenagers

The world of teenagers and preteens revolves around their friends. Let your children include their friends as much as you can without totally compromising your family time. They are at the onset of adolescence, when peer influence begins to rival and often surpass that of parents. Choose your battles wisely, and keep in mind that, during certain periods of adolescence especially, your children's friends have an incredible amount of power. If you've been able to establish open and honest communication with a child of this age, you'll be at a tremendous advantage here. Set a positive example by your own behavior, and let your kids know what's expected.

If your kids are keeping unsavory company, you have to find a way to discourage without *forbidding*. When you forbid your children to see certain friends, you only make them more appealing. Note the Romeo-and-Juliet effect here. You may be tempted to be the cool mom who has rules that are lax and allows kids the run of the house. As much as you want to be their friend, you are first their parent—step or otherwise—and you represent security and stability.

Get to Know Other Parents

Get to know the parents of your children's friends. When you have an ally and the parents all stick together with rules and expectations, life can be a lot easier. If your son or daughter is invited to a party and you haven't met the parents, follow them up to the door when you drop them off. Kids may be somewhat embarrassed by this, depending upon how it's handled, but hold your ground and let them know you care about where they are and who they spend time with.

Keep a Watchful Eye

As much as you may crave peace and quiet, it's safer when the kids are at your house and you can monitor what goes one. As we said, observe, don't hover. Raising kids to be responsible and safe in today's world is a huge challenge. You will be fighting more demons than you ever imagined.

Breaking the Rules

You and your husband need to support one another and present a united front. If the kids break the rules while playing with friends, they'll have to pay the consequences. You can discipline and set standards with love. Though you might hear "I hate you" once or twice (or ten times), they will know the difference. It's hard to explain the difference between control freak and responsible parent to an angry child. At those moments, it's easy to give in, and so hard to say no. But you and your partner should stand your ground and do what's best for the child. Sometimes that's learning that rules can't be broken.

"My House Is Grand Central Station!"

When you encourage your kids to have friends over and be socially interactive, you run the risk of compromising your own privacy and solitude. This goes with the territory of marrying someone with children. If you don't think you can handle the loss of space and privacy, we encourage you to take another look at your situation before you say "I do." This does *not* have to be a negative for you. Activity and positive energy throughout the household can be a stimulating and wonderful lifestyle. You just have to remember to set fair and reasonable limits and work within the confines of your family's needs.

Kids need to be able to feel that their friends are welcome. Do they have the run of the entire house? Of course not. There are certain areas that remain off limits to visitors. Do you set standards and expectations for behavior? Of course you do. Your values as a person, as a couple, and as a family should be followed when you have guests in your home. But allow some of your resoluteness to ease and realize that everyone has individual patterns of behavior. Again, monitor without hovering, and respect the fact that this is your stepchildren's home as well as your own. You knew that when you married your husband, and you want it to be a safe comfortable haven for your whole family.

We know there are so many things to think about when you marry someone with children. Getting it all to balance and work out may take a while. It's a learning experience for all of you. Remember the terms *patience, respect, communication,* and *compromise.* After they all grow up and leave for college, you may look at your husband and say, "It's way too quiet in here." And you may quietly add, "At last!"

Curfews

How you and your partner handle curfews is vital and serves as an index of your parenting style in general. We could not feel more strongly about this, as so many parent/child problems start here. Sadly, some parents just do not concern themselves about what their kids do when away from home. At times, they are so disabled by their own shortcomings or issues that they are simply unable to involve themselves in this crucial area of their children's lives. Not infrequently, the teenage child becomes "parentified" and assumes the role of the parent in the home if no one else can.

The requirement of being home at certain times embodies the concepts of power and self-control. So often, adolescents want to believe they have the wings to fly alone. Typically, however, they do not have the wisdom or experience to do so and often find themselves crashing in one way or another. Though they may not (okay, do not) directly admit to it, kids appreciate the time and effort parents spend devising reasonable curfew rules. Curfews are generally viewed by kids as an index of parental caring. If they have a curfew, that means their parents care where they are and when they come home. Kids want and need structure. They are often uncomfortable without it.

The younger the child, the more specific and concrete the guidelines must be. Here are some suggestions for establishing and managing an effective curfew system:

- Curfew rules, as with morning rising, mealtime, homework, and social issues, should be generated and approved by both biological parents. If both birth parents provide input—and are willing to make needed compromises—they will be much more likely to cooperatively monitor and enforce the agreement. This will eliminate arguments like, "When I'm at my mom's, I get to stay out later." This cooperation between biological parents goes a long way to counter kids who test the limits and/or play one parent against another, which virtually all kids attempt. Stepmoms, too, might be asked to offer suggestions here as to what might have worked for her own kids, or for other moms and/or stepmoms she might know.

- Kids should be allowed input. Typically, at the age of about nine or ten, kids like to have a voice in issues of where and how they spend their time. If allowed input, kids will be more likely to adhere to ground rules. Parents should retain the veto power, however, as this is one issue not open to a majority vote.
- Curfew rules should be clear and specific as to times to be home on school nights, weekends, and special occasions.
- Be sure kids know that they have to check in with the parents they're staying with whenever they're out. There should be dialogue between parents and children regarding where the children are, whom they are with, and what they are doing. In this age of cell phones, this should be easy enough. If the child must be unavoidably late, explanations should always be provided beforehand to parents via phone.
- Consequences of missing curfew should also be clear and agreed upon up front by all parties. Kids, when given input as to type of consequences deserved, are more likely to accept and comply. Interestingly, when given input and choices, they are often more stringent in disciplining themselves than are their parents.

Setting and enforcing a curfew is likely an area that will cause some strife, especially at first. Be sure you, your partner, and the biological mother are consistent in your enforcement of the rules. Expect some fights, but reassure yourself that you're doing the right thing for the child.

Bedtime Battles

When to go to bed and how to manage bedtime routines is another arena of potential conflict. Once again, it is vitally important to initiate common and specific ground rules between Mom's house and Dad's house, particularly if there are frequent visitations or a joint custody situation is in place.

In younger children, bedtimes bring out such issues as, "I'm older now and should be able to stay up later!" (even though the same child might be simultaneously yawning and glassy-eyed with fatigue). Older children are, of course, capable of handling increasingly later betimes. Assuming that some agreed-upon bedtime plans have been previously established by the biological parents and children themselves for the various nights during the week, try these helpful tips:

- Define what going to bed really means. Does it mean being physically in bed? Does it mean allowing TV and iPods in operation? Or, does it just signal the beginning of bedtime preparations as outlined below? Or, are there other ideas as to what bedtime is?
- Provide a reminder twenty or thirty minutes before the zero hour that bedtime preparations need to begin. This makes the transition less abrupt and demanding and invites greater compliance.
- Specify necessary bedtime preparations, such as hair washing, teeth brushing, showers, the laying out of school clothing and more.
- Determine allowable bedtime rituals and their time allotments, including when lights, TVs, iPods, cell phones, and computers are to be turned off and in what order.
- Will there be a goodnight bedroom check by the dad or stepmom? If so, this should occur at the mom's house as

well. Age level is obviously an issue here. Whatever is agreed upon should be consistently followed.

As with any other challenge, bedtimes will go more smoothly if you think through what needs to happen and are clear with the child about your expectations.

Recommended Reading

Throughout this chapter, we've stressed again and again the importance of generating mutually accepted rules regarding when to get out of bed, mealtimes, homework, friendship issues, curfews, and bedtimes. Kids growing up with chaos will live chaotically. Kids growing up in an orderly environment will live life in an orderly and purposeful manner. The most comprehensive treatment of establishing house rules we've seen is that presented by Isolina Ricci, in her book, *Mom's House, Dad's House*. We consider it essential reading when it comes to this issue.

A Case in Point: Being on the Same Page

Elaine told us that she had always loved to cook. Living alone with her ten-year-old son didn't give her much of an opportunity to show off her talents, and they frequently dined out since it was just the two of them. When she married a man with custody of two teenage sons and a seven-year-old daughter, she was excited to be able to spend time in a kitchen and fix meals the whole family could enjoy.

Of course, it was immediately a disaster. "The boys grabbed food when they wanted it or fixed pizza and nachos. His daughter didn't like anything I fixed and wanted fast food every night. My husband didn't seem to know what to do and was always handing out money to someone to go get food. He did this even after I'd spent time in the kitchen fixing a nutritious meal. I was so angry, and it caused a lot of problems. My own son was angry that my stepchildren treated me with so little respect, as even he noticed it."

Elaine and her husband had to have some serious conversations about what their expectations for mealtime were and had to promise to present a united front. That was the first and most essential step to resolving what had become a huge issue in the family. Elaine went to great lengths to ask the children what they would like her to fix and what foods they enjoyed. It was a frustrating task on her part, because she just expected them to be grateful to have someone cooking for them. If you know kids, they don't always respond the way we think they should.

Her husband agreed *not* to dole out money for pizza or fast food if the kids didn't like what Elaine prepared for dinner. They didn't have to eat it, but they were responsible for taking care of their own needs if they didn't. Elaine did her best to fix what they said they liked and even let the kids take turns deciding the menu. She encouraged her stepdaughter to help her fix meals and had in-house cooking lessons with the boys.

"Is it perfect? No. Is it better? Yes. The family has really done a 180 since Jeff and I decided that we would lay down some basic expectations and behavior of our own. We actually sit down together at mealtime as much as we can. Two years ago, I would have told you this would never happen. My feelings can still get hurt, but it's much less often, and I don't get angry anymore. I've learned that the world of teenagers will probably never be what you think it should. I guess I forgot what it was like to be one myself."

Good for Elaine for hanging in there. By the time the boys leave home, her own son and stepdaughter will be heading into their teenage years. Experience will be on her side then!

REFLECTIONS: KEY ISSUES IN CHAPTER 8

- Merging your customs with those of his kids takes assessment, preplanning with their biological mom, compromise, and patience.

- Ask kids their food preferences. Acknowledge up front that you will try, but that you may not be able to exactly duplicate their biological mom's cooking.

- Help his kids schedule time for homework and avoid procrastination. Volunteer to help, especially in the areas of your expertise.

- Get to know their friends' parents. Communicate and cooperate with them in knowing where kids are, what they are doing, and whom they are with.

- Create a home in which kids are comfortable. But ground rules are especially important here. Adults must be present for monitoring and mentoring.

- Curfews are crucial. Time plans and consequences should be consistent in both homes.

- Bedtime battles can be won with reminders and consistently defined steps at both Dad and Mom's house.

Chapter 9

Disciplining Stepkids

Battle-tested stepmoms acknowledge that disciplining their stepkids is a significant source of tension in their families. Disciplining presents some of the most difficult, anxiety-provoking, and confusing challenges, our stepmoms report. The adage, "blood is thicker than water" was never truer. But fear not. We'll share tactics from experienced veterans so you can hit the ground running.

Think about it. Military strategists would deem it foolhardy to make a landing and try to secure a beachhead on foreign territory without some advance intelligence reports. Likewise, you want to be sure you have as much information as you can get before moving in. Key to this venture are your knowledge of each kid's personality, their dynamics as a group, and their relationship to their father. (See Chapter 1 for a refresher on getting to know the kids.) Don't make baseless presumptions about who they are and how they might react to you. Even more importantly—be an observer and advisor, not an authoritarian, for a good while *after* you move in. There is good reason for this, we promise.

"You're Not My Mom!"

You're really not, you see. You didn't birth and rear them from infancy. You do not yet have that bonding history with them. So, if you hear declarations of this type, do your best to understand and don't take it personally. I know, easier said than done. You need time and patience to show them that you sincerely care and that you're in it for the long term. Stepmoms suggest that this may take as long as eighteen months to two years from the day you meet them! Why? Daddy may have had a series of relationships that went by the wayside. Perhaps some of them were only a few months in duration. His kids might well wonder how long you will be in the picture. Thus, building trust takes time. Obviously, their age makes a difference. Little ones attach more quickly, while adolescents are more wary. It's preferable, of course, if they have met you prior to moving in together. This allows your relationship to develop a running start.

So you're not their mom, but neither are you the maid. You are in the process of rising in rank. Dad must take the leading role at this point—he outranks you. It is best to step back and look on for a bit right now. If your role at this point seems frustrating, unclear, and cloudy, join the club. Those feelings are totally normal at this stage. Sensing that his kids were also confused at this point, one open and honest Dad announced, "I know that things are confusing to all of us now. That's pretty normal. We're all in this together and we'll work it out together. I'd like your ideas on the subject."

Establishing Rules

Before stepkids adopt negative habits like leaving messes in the family room for everyone to step around, you and your partner need to establish some basic rules of the house.

Outlining appropriate behaviors from the get-go is much easier than trying to change long-standing habits. You two should set forth all rules in a united stance. (Review Chapter 8 regarding curfews and bedtimes.)

Who's Moving Where?

The situation is different, of course, depending on whether the family will now live in your home, a new home, or their home. If the move is into their home, it is more likely that many behaviors have already been established. If change is necessary, you can assume that it will take longer. The kids may view doing certain things in certain ways as their right. If the move is into your home, you may value the sanctity of certain areas and items. Why does living space matter? Because you'll have to take precedence into account when you set or change rules.

Where Do We Start?

When you set rules, enlist input from his kids and your kids. Again, when all have input, all are more likely to comply. As always, you and your partner retain veto power. Certainly, the same rules should apply for all children whether "his," "hers," or "ours." Make your rules specific and clear so that there is no controversy as to which behaviors are in compliance and which are not. As with any other rule, they can be modified if you and your partner agree on it.

Try not to begin with too many rules. Should the need arise, rules can be added. We talked about rules regarding getting up in the morning, mealtime behaviors, homework, socializing with friends, curfews, and bedtimes in Chapter 8. Other items that may need immediate attention include:

- Assigned chores and responsibilities
- Participation in family functions
- Pet care
- Money issues
- Modesty/privacy
- Dating
- Computer/Internet usage

Be sure you give the kids a reason for each established rule. For example, "Hang up clean clothes in your closet or fold them in your bureau. Put dirty clothes in your hamper—do not leave them lying on the floor or on the furniture of any room. That way, your clothes will not be damaged, lost, or in anybody's way." The message here is that everyone's rights (to clean clothes and a clean house) and belongings (their clothes) are being protected.

Whose Word Is Final?

If you disagree with the kids' biological mother about a rule (or consequence or reward), you're in a tough spot. Generally, we feel that biological parents of the child in question should make the final judgment in establishing a system of rules (and rewards and consequences). The same is true regarding system modifications, ambiguities as to whether a rule is broken, and if a reward or consequence should be dispensed. You can serve as an advisor and offer suggestions and ideas. If you vehemently disagree, state your reasoning (which will, of course, have the best interest of the kids first and foremost). If your husband and the biological mom still feel the rule needs to be as is, get on board and enforce it. Revisit it later if necessary, away from the children.

Use Appropriate Rewards

Research has long told us that giving rewards or positive reinforcement to encourage good behavior is more effective than punishment for negative behaviors. In most situations, however, you'll need to use some combination of both rewards and consequences. Let's first address developing a reward system.

Should We Really Use Rewards?

Often, parents will have one or more of the following objections to the use of rewards:

1. Some view giving rewards as bribing.
2. Others ask if they will have to provide the reward from now on.
3. Still others frown and state that when they were young, they willingly completed the same tasks and didn't expect to be rewarded.
4. Finally, certain parents question whether it's fair to give one child a reward while his or her sibling does it with no reward.

In summary, some parents' implicit opinion seems to be, "Why can't kids be good for nothing?" (Pun intended.) All of the above views are understandable. We know, however, that structuring a reward system can be powerfully effective. We've seen it work wonders. Does it always work? Unfortunately, no. Let's look at each of these concerns.

1. **Isn't it bribery?** No. If the child is involved in selecting the reward and the system is carefully planned and carried out by both parents and child, it is not bribing.

2. **Will we have to give the reward forever?** Nope. You can phase out the token reward (be it money, a special privilege, or redeemable stars on a chart) when the *social* rewards kick in. Social rewards include praise and approval from teachers, peers, and parents for improved grades and/or behavior. For example, say Johnny needs to stop hitting other kids. When he stops hitting, Johnny's peers may say, "Hey, you're not a mean kid after all." Teachers now smile approvingly. The child is now pleased and proud, and likes the feeling of resolving fights without hitting. Results lead to an enhanced self-concept.

3. *I never got these kinds of rewards!* Well, that's too bad. It's still a good idea for your kids today. Giving a specific reward should be viewed as priming the pump or as a starter. You're preparing them to do even greater things.

4. **But my other stepkid does that without a reward!** That's okay. Even if other siblings currently do a task without a specific reward, we're willing to bet that these children have *other* behaviors that they could improve and for which a reward system would be effective. That should take care of the fairness aspect.

The Right Way to Reward

Rewards are only useful when instituted properly. First off, only use one reward program at a time. You want the child to focus on the important problem at hand and resolve it. Follow these steps for an effective reward system:

1. **Identify the exact behavior to be improved and be sure the goal is accomplishable.** The child's progress should be observable and easily measurable so

you can determine whether she's made improvements. For example, raising a grade in a given subject from an F to a C would be a measurable behavior, and, more than likely, capable of being accomplished.

2. **Parents, with the child's input, should specify what the reward is.** Some children are motivated by earning a special privilege. Others are attracted to monetary rewards. For example, giving one reward unit for raising an F to a C and perhaps two units or more for greater improvements may be appropriate. The key is that the child must want the reward and you must approve of it. (The most frequent mistake by parents is giving too much.)

3. **Set up an initial trial period.** Both parents and child should agree that there will be an initial experimental period, say one or two weeks, during which the system needs to be evaluated to see if the type and amount of reward are appropriate and effective. Necessary adjustments should then be made.

4. **Make weekly charts to record amount of progress and rewards earned.** This helps kids see that they're improving (or not) and shows them how close they are to their goal.

5. **Have an end in mind.** The system should be phased down or out when it is obvious that the new and improved behavior is well established and maintained via social rewards. You can then start a new reward program for another issue if necessary.

Of course, continue to bestow rewards and gifts in the traditional sense for notable achievements and special occasions—exceptional academic and extracurricular achievements, graduations, birthdays, holidays, and marriage.

Create Appropriate Consequences

What type of teacher, manager, and/or boss would you like to have? If you said one who understands you, cares about you, listens to you, considers your input, and is firm and fair to all, you're not alone. Your kids want the same characteristics in their parents.

Besides all those things, you'll also need to be assertive and act with authority during crises, but not be an authoritarian. Yes, it's an overwhelming list! And you won't accomplish it all overnight. Remember that 91-pound, elderly, gray-haired teacher in whose classroom you could hear a pin drop when she spoke? Why could she command that order? Because she was respected and walked the walk she talked. Everyone knew her reputation. Like her, you'll need to earn that reputation over time.

Use this list to establish fair and effective consequences for unacceptable behavior:

- You and your partner should determine specific consequences ahead of time, with input from the children.
- Consequences should relate to the infraction. For example, if your teenager comes in one hour late, his curfew for the next outing might be one hour earlier for five days.
- Consequences, like rewards, should be specific and measurable. Time periods should be fixed and definite. For example, you could restrict or limit the use of a cell phone and iPod for two weeks.
- If possible, build in an option of "time off for good behavior." For example, if your daughter is to be grounded for ten days, allow her to work off up to four days by completing some extra tasks beyond those she normally does.
- Never issue a consequence to all children because of the misdeed(s) of one. No child should be responsible for the

behavior of a sibling or stepsibling. Encouragement and support of each other is always a great thing, but never should a child be held accountable or punished for the intended actions of another.

What Happens at "Her" House?

If you've already established good cooperation, communication, and involvement with their birth mom from the beginning, dealing with discipline will be much easier. Both parties will be more likely to stick to the same regulations, rewards, and consequences no matter where the kids are. They won't have time to fall into bad habits because the same standards will be applied all the time. Again, greater involvement by all leads to greater compliance by all. Keep these two things in mind:

1. Monitoring and enforcement are vital. Great planning without follow-through won't work. Be sure consequences are implemented no matter where the infraction happened.
2. Continue your open and honest communication with her.

The focus, as always, needs to be on the children's welfare, not on unresolved conflicts between parents. In fact, we've seen animosity between parents disappear when both come to appreciate the common ground of working together for their children's betterment.

Who Disciplines Whom?

Okay, now you've got rules, rewards, and consequences clearly outlined for all kids at all locations. Who handles the implementation? Most of our respondents suggest that your husband should discipline his kids, you should take care of yours, and both of you should participate equally in disciplining children that you have together. We agree in principle, but realistically, we know there will be instances where you have to be the sergeant at arms for whatever children are in front of you—perhaps sooner than you would hope.

Treat Each Kid the Same

Most of us, to be honest, have a positive bias toward our own biological children. Why? Because of our long history with them. They are our creation. We have invested countless hours, weeks, and years in molding them. Have you ever given requested changes to another's writing or artwork? It's often taken rather personally. (We know, because we've secured opinions from other professionals while writing this book.)

It's the same when he tries to make an objective appraisal of his own kids. They've come from another environmental and genetic structure, which may not jive with yours. They are his creation, in which he takes pride and for which he may feel guilty because their lives have been disrupted. As a result, he may fear offending them and is reluctant to say "No" to them. The result is that they become spoiled.

Regardless of your biases and his, you should show no differences in caring for, rewarding, and issuing consequences to his kids, your kids, or the kids you've had together. This is a goal; it won't happen overnight. What do you do when biases show themselves from time to time? The best antidote is to be honest. Acknowledge your biases and pledge to become as fair as you can as quickly as you can. This helps his kids to understand your predicament and your humanness. They will respect your openness, honesty, and efforts to be objective and fair. Might they attempt to use this information on occasion as a manipulative device? Of course.

Now, about his kids specifically. "I just can't understand them," you say? Well, you're right; you can't. You don't know them yet. And you can't love someone you don't know. You need time to pass in order to develop these relationships. During that time, you should:

1. Withhold fixed judgments
2. Appreciate from whence they came
3. See how they react to a number of life situations

Remember that if you're looking for negative issues, you'll find them. Conversely, if you look for the positive, you will find that as well. The key is to identify the positive and build on that.

The Kids' Video Game Mindset: There's Only Winning and Losing

Like it or not, video games are here to stay. There are the good guys, the bad guys, the battle, and the outcome. Someone definitely wins and someone definitely loses. Lots of parents disapprove of the violence often portrayed, which can encourage aggression. Our real point, however, is that video-game usage influences kids to think in black and white terms—that is, winning or losing. This mindset influences the establishment of rules, rewards, and consequences in a very real way.

So much of life deals with shades of gray. We all must learn to deal with the gray and the ambiguous. You'll no doubt face ethical dilemmas as to what is right or wrong. Are white lies ever okay? Should extenuating circumstances ever be considered? What if your child was late for curfew because she was truly helping a friend in crisis and forgot to call you? What if you could not follow through on a promise because of a similar reason? You and your children need to learn to tackle the ambiguous, the shades of gray, and make the best judgments for all concerned. We can't give you step-by-step directions on how to do that—of course, it's not that simple. You need to rely on the trust you're building with his kids, your gut feelings, and open and honest communication to help guide you. Make sure you discuss this with your husband to be certain that you agree on the right approach and judgments.

Ongoing Maintenance of the Rules, Rewards, and Consequences

Rules, rewards, and consequences might be very clear and fair, with agreement and involvement from all key parties. But, they will collapse if broken rules go unnoticed, if promised rewards are not given, or an infraction occurs without consequences or appropriate consequences. The best of systems do not run by themselves! They need to be monitored and enforced on a continual basis and modified if necessary. A system not monitored is no system at all. Be sure you follow through on your program.

Disagreements Between You and Your Partner

As we said, rules jointly established should be jointly enforced. Kids are geniuses at spotting even subtle conflict between you and their father. In time, you'll probably notice differences in how you and your partner interpret whether a rule is broken or how you determine the amount, type, and extent of consequences. Never question your partner's judgment in front of the child. Settle the disagreements in private between stepmom and dad (and biological mom if need be) before presenting decisions to the children themselves.

On occasion, you may disagree with Dad in favor of the child in terms of a reduced consequence. He can then indicate to the child that you have convinced him to lighten the punishment. As a result, the child might see you as an ally and as genuinely interested in his or her welfare.

When One Parent Is Away

At times, it might be necessary for you, the stepmom, to be in charge. (It may even happen much sooner than the ideal eighteen to twenty-four months of apprenticing as a parent.) Dad might be called away on business or to attend an emergency family matter or for whatever reason. If this is necessary, Dad should clearly point out to his kids that while he is gone you will enforce the rules. He should assure them that he will support your decisions. If necessary, he can "rule" on certain ambiguous instances when he returns. And, of course, circumstances may necessitate your absence from your new family as well. Now Dad is in charge. All of the precautions for stepmoms being away now apply to Dad. He might just need a briefing on issues he doesn't usually handle.

Be Consistent

A key to successful implementation of rules is to enforce them consistently. If certain behaviors merit rewards or consequences today, they should do the same tomorrow. Inconsistency fosters confusion and provokes remarks like, "But you didn't say anything when I did that yesterday!" or "How come Sarah got away with it and I didn't?" These problems and more can result from a lack of consistency. Sometimes it's difficult to be "the bad guy" and enforce the rules all the time, but you'll be glad you did when your household is running smoothly.

Special Teenage Issues

So he has teenage children? Or they will be in a couple of years? You may be wondering what kind of discipline issues you'll face with teens.

Why Are They the Way They Are?

Let's first discuss the many life changes teenagers are beset with—in addition to their dad's divorce from their mom. Here are a few of the most significant:

- **The adolescent growth spurt:** It begins with most girls at about age ten and with most boys at about age twelve. Generally, girls will be taller, heavier, and stronger than boys for several years. There are wide variations as to just when the growth spurt may happen. This can result in a reduced self-image for a time.
- **Sexual maturation occurs:** This includes enlargement of sexual organs, first appearance of sperm, beginning of menstruation, breast development, hormonal changes, pubic and underarm hair, increased width of pelvis, broadening of shoulders, as well as voice and skin changes. This ushers in questions about "What's happening to me?" Again, there are variations as to beginning times from one individual to another.

- **Greater tendency to take risks:** This may result in increased incidence of serious injuries due to accidents.
- **Concern with appearance and body image:** Social stress and vulnerability to eating disorders, alcohol, drugs, and sexual activity emerge.
- **Heightened egocentrism:** Perhaps because of some of the foregoing issues and their increased ability to think abstractly, adolescents frequently manifest increased argumentativeness, fault finding, indecision, and a feeling of being bulletproof, thinking they are somehow magically protected from auto accidents, addictions, and becoming pregnant.
- **A search for identity:** Questions of, "Who am I?" and "Where am I going?" are central. Abrupt changes of temperament may occur as a result as they "try out" different modes of behavior.

So many of these issues are related to teens' uncertainty about how they will fit in socially, emotionally, physically, and vocationally. If a teen says nasty things to you and others, it's probably a projection of his or her own insecurity. Acting super cool, dressing differently, and being slovenly on occasion are almost always teens' attempts to disguise discomfort.

Now for the Good News

His teenager may discover that you are "the adult who really understands me." He or she can be genuinely sweet, charming, cooperative, and helpful. He or she may well share with you issues they would never share with either biological parent. Many of our interviewed stepmoms continue to carry out lifelong relations with stepchildren long after they've left the nest.

(Yes, that *was* a short section. We didn't say there was a *lot* of good news.)

Tips for Dealing with Teens

Because of the special challenges in dealing with teenagers, you'll need an arsenal of tips such as those that follow. Review, as well, suggestions in Chapter 1, Meeting His Kids and Building Relationships.

- **Gauge moods.** As your teen enters the room after having been gone, take his emotional temperature. If he looks tense and angry, provide a suggestion for him to relax, such as a shower, taking a walk, or other exercise. Listen if he wants to talk. Toss out a conversational hook having to do with one of his interests or activities. This is not a time to explain house rules.
- **Allow teenagers privacy.** Knock before entering their rooms. Their journals, letters, and writings are for their eyes only.
- **Spend special time with each one alone.** Reflect their feelings in a nonjudgmental way.
- **Don't take unkind remarks seriously.** It usually means, "Keep your distance right now." Don't be disappointed if you don't feel a lot of appreciation or affection at these times.
- **Don't pressure them for appreciation or affection.** They're sort of like puppies that have been spooked. Let them come to you in their own time.
- **Be yourself.** They can spot faking like blinking lights on a radar screen. Don't talk in a language or act in such a way that's not you.
- **Suggest that their father** (if he has not already done so) assure them that no one can replace them in his life.
- **Use "I" messages rather than "you" messages.** For example, if the teen deliberately defied you, say something

like, "I was disappointed when you did that," as opposed to, "You were really mean today."

A Case in Point: Not My Job

Barbara, a well-intentioned lady, moved into Jim's house soon after their marriage. Jim had primary custody of his fifteen-year-old twin boys, Tim and Tom. Although Jim was a caring father and provided well for his sons, he was reluctant to ask them to take any responsibilities in and about the house. Barbara willingly did most of the household cooking and cleaning in addition to her own job. The boys did very little to help and expected someone else to pick up after them. The boys increasingly came to regard Barbara as their live-in servant. One afternoon, Tim, while slouched on the sofa watching TV, yelled, "Barb, get me a Coke and two or three cookies."

A couple of days later, Baxter, the family dog, whom the boys previously took care of, made a mess on the off-white family-room carpet. Returning from work to again find the boys watching TV, Barbara observed, "I see Baxter's mess is still there." Tom replied, "Yeah, that's your job, Barb," not taking his eyes off the TV screen.

Barbara's situation required some serious family meetings regarding the responsibilities of each household member. She told the boys she was happy to do things for them if the relationship was reciprocal. She was by no means their servant and maid. Once she and her husband were on the same page and she was sure of his support, she held her ground and let the boys know what she expected of them. Although it was difficult, she continued to treat them with respect and in a nurturing manner. Many would have walked out the door, but Barbara honored her commitment to the man she married and to her new family.

REFLECTIONS: KEY ISSUES IN CHAPTER 9

- You're really not their mom; but you're not the maid either.

- Establishing rules, rewards, and consequences requires input from the dad, stepmom, biological mom, and kids.

- You must monitor and enforce rules, reward systems, and consequences consistently for them to be effective.

- Ideally, his kids, your kids, and the kids you have together should be treated the same. But recognize the difficulties here and be honest with them.

- Younger kids tend to see things as black or white and have trouble dealing with ambiguities in making judgments.

- Discuss differences in judgment in private with your husband. Present a united and mutually supportive stance.

- Be aware of the tremendous changes with which teens are dealing. Many of their responses result from a projection onto you of their own frustrations.

- Teenage stepkids are involved in complex physical and emotional changes and may therefore pose special challenges.

Chapter 10

Basic Duties and Responsibilities

Ah, the division of household chores—surely you've discussed this issue amid the romantic fervor, right? No?
Well, we'll tackle it here. Adding kids to the mix can introduce chaos to the just-tidied-up bedrooms, bathroom, family room, and kitchen. And what if stepmom works outside
the home? Can dad boil water, vacuum, and clean the toilet?
Will he? Who will squire the kids to school functions and
monitor homework and curfews? Ambiguity, unfortunately,
usually means the rookie stepmom gets to do it.

As with most things, running a household and keeping
everything humming takes a cooperative effort. Let's hope
your new husband doesn't just assume you're going to do it
all. Unless, of course, you prefer working outside the home
all day and then like a field hand at home all night. Even
if this is the way you begin, we think you'll soon tire of
including "maid" as one of your job responsibilities along
with cooking and childcare. Talk about it beforehand and at
length. Whatever you decide, everyone needs to do his or
her part, including the children.

Domestics: Cooking, Cleaning, Clothing Care

Today's families live a much different life than did our parents and grandparents. Some very traditional families remain where all domestic duties are the woman's responsibility alone, but for most families, things have drastically changed in that arena. Cooking used to belong exclusively to Mom, but more and more dads are contributing to and sharing in that task, if not taking over completely. It's usually Dad we see standing over the grill in the backyard, as well as waving the meat fork. The bottom line with all domestic chores: Enlist help, be organized, and do what works for your family.

Don't Do It All Yourself

There is no reason that you should have to do the cooking, laundry, and cleaning all on your own. If you don't work outside the home, you might have more time and inclination to take over the majority of the domestic tasks, but by no means should it be solely your responsibility. Perhaps you two would like to share the cooking duties. But if you love to cook and prepare meals, take it over and cook the majority of the time. If you work outside the home and have career obligations similar to your husband, then all things in the home need to be shared as equally as possible. If you can afford a cleaning service, consider that as an option. Even with a weekly cleaning service, you'll still find plenty of daily chores and upkeep that need to be done. It seems that this frequently falls on the woman; perhaps this is because she does so many things automatically.

If you are racing around picking up after people and trying to make sure everyone is fed on time, you won't even have time to take care of yourself. The key for you is effectively delegating responsibility—to everyone else who lives in the house, including the kids (we'll get to that topic shortly).

Pick Your Battles

We know some kids are notoriously sloppy, and their bedrooms are a disaster. You nag and nag and get ignored. Our best advice is to choose your battles. If your kid's room is a mess, just keep the door shut. If you insist, for example, that their rooms must harbor no food, dirty dishes, or wet towels, that might be a good compromise. Don't drive yourself nuts over the state of their rooms. Go in and clean periodically if you can't stand it; otherwise, there are bigger fish to fry elsewhere—namely, the shared spaces in the home.

You have the right to expect certain standards in the parts of the house shared by the whole family. For example, if your teens do their own laundry (we hope), ask them not to leave clothes in the washer and dryer for hours or days on end. Essentially, when their behaviors and habits affect the rest of the family in any way, it has to be in a considerate and respectful manner.

Involving the Kids

It's pretty simple: kids who live in your house should contribute to its upkeep. So many moms and stepmoms told us they just do it themselves because it's easier than constantly nagging or reminding their children. This is an age-old problem and nothing new to any of us. Still, when kids contribute in some fashion to the home and family, they will take more pride in being a part of it. Here are some ways to give everyone the best chance at success:

1. Be sure you and your partner agree on the details of giving your kids chores: what will be done, how often, rewards, and consequences. Your united front and consistent enforcement will show the kids you mean business.

2. Take into account their free time and schedules. If an older child has sports practice on weeknights, give her chores to do on weekends. If a child is having a tough time with a particular class, give him a short reprieve on his chores so he can spend more time on his homework.

3. Make a list of tasks that need attention and post it in a central location. Let the kids know that you expect them to complete certain of them. No, you're not asking too much of them—on the contrary, you're offering them valuable learning experiences.

4. Ask everyone to choose a chore or two from the list. First volunteers get first choices. As you can guess, certain tasks are just more interesting and rewarding than others, so those will be picked first and you'll need to assign the leftovers that no one wants. Tell everyone that you will rotate tasks at regular intervals so no one is stuck with a particular chore forever.

5. Announce to the kids that if they do their chores properly and in a timely manner, the rewards can be privileges, allowances, freedom, cell phones, or whatever you deem suitable. If they don't follow through, they will face consequences.

We know this sounds easier than it is, and we're not trying to simplify the process of getting kids to take responsibility for chores at home. Remember to set a good example, and *make sure you and your husband agree and are on the same page.*

Busy Teens and Chores

As kids grow up, they should obviously take more responsibility for things at home. Letting kids drift through life without contributing in any way to the family and being responsible for certain components of the home and family life is a recipe for disaster. If you want each person in the family to take ownership, then, as kids get older, they need to be responsible for more assigned chores or duties.

Many parents say their older kids are too busy with school, extracurricular activities, and jobs to do anything at home other than eat and sleep. That may be very true. You have to set your own priorities and guidelines and determine what's acceptable to you and your partner. If getting good grades, staying busy with the band or sports, and working at a fast-food joint are contribution enough for you, that's fine—as long as you both agree. Teens face a lot of pressure today, and being a good student and contributing member of the school community are, of course, positive and admirable traits.

Pass on Handy Skills to Kids

We've talked a few times about how stepparents may possess skills that biological parents do not. Think about that again when it comes to chores. Could you teach a child a skill while he does chores? For example, basic carpentry and plumbing, woodworking, sewing, cooking, computer repair, animal care, and gardening and landscaping are all examples of skills yielding lifelong benefits to children and, in turn, to their own children one day. You'll also facilitate parent-child bonding (but don't tell the kids that). How should you start? Simply ask a child to help you with any task needing attention. Kids have a way of getting caught up and hooked on the process. Being involved in this way provides them with hands-on experience with ongoing family responsibilities.

Kids do have busy schedules, and you do your best to accommodate them and help them meet their needs. But you can't be the one doing all of the giving without expecting something in return. If they can't do chores, they should at least contribute respect, civility, and gratitude to the rest of the household.

Paying Kids to Do Chores

Right after you've assigned your children chores, they're likely to ask "How much do we get paid?" Though this decision is up to you and your partner, we don't believe in paying kids for standard jobs around the house, unless it is something beyond the daily or weekly regimen or having to do with a specific behavior modification plan. (Obviously, if you expect your sixteen-year-old to power-wash the house, that calls for a little compensation.)

If you do choose to pay your kids, have a short- and long-term plan in mind ahead of time. Decide what will induce a "raise" and when they're eligible. Keep in mind that kids' financial needs increase as they get older, but they can't simply expect that you'll give them more money for doing the same number of chores. Everyone works in the family. Each person has a role to play and some kind of contribution to make. Compensation should be in proportion to the contribution made and not just automatic. Also, if you decide to pay them for chores, use it as an opportunity to teach kids about the value of money and earning it yourself. Ask them to let you know if they want to buy something. If you're okay with the purchase, you can figure out a way together to accommodate them within the limits of your budget and responsibility as a parent. After all, we appreciate more what we ourselves have earned. Kids can learn that at an early age. For example, if a child wants to buy a new video game, consider providing opportunities for him to make extra money around the house. You want to avoid teaching them to take the things you buy for them for granted.

House, Lawn, and Garden Maintenance

Leaky faucets to fix, rooms to paint, drapes to hang, roofs to caulk, garages to reorganize, bulbs to plant—and neither you nor your new husband has a green thumb or knows a slot head from a Phillips. Avoid that situation by having a casual but specific conversation with him early on about his skills and how you'll handle home maintenance. You can get a sense of how adept he is by asking him to help you with one of these tasks at your abode before you two move in together. Or offer to help him fix something at his pad—again, before the two of you move in together. Since you can pretty much bet that his maintenance will repeat itself, you'll get a realistic sense of what he can and will do later on.

Knowing his habits in advance prevents later disappointments. Maybe your own father and/or a former significant other is Mr. Super Fix-it. It's easy to expect every man to be a carbon copy, but that's not always the case. Maybe you are the mechanical whiz of the family and can repair anything with chewing gum and a paper clip, while he might be a supersweet ideal mate in every other way but can't change a light bulb. That's fine, as long as you know what to expect rather than waiting forever for the new shelves to be hung.

If neither of you is handy, compile a list of reputable repair services. That's what those companies are there for!

Automobile Servicing: Yours and His

Next to your residence, you're probably most dependent on your car. It usually constitutes your second greatest expense as well, so you need to be sure someone's taking care of its upkeep.

Insurance

No matter how many cars the family owns, be sure that you have insurance in place for each vehicle and that it's in the name of the vehicle owner(s). If not, clear these issues up as soon as possible. States typically require some evidence of vehicle insurance or the ability to post a certain bond amount. Consult with your insurance agent regarding the details of your coverage, including deductible amounts should you be involved in an accident and which drivers are registered on which cars (including children of driving age). Often, your old policies may not be suitable for your current needs.

Maintenance

Today's cars, though very reliable, still need regular servicing and care. Oil changes and lubrication every 3,000 to 5,000 miles, tire rotation, balancing and pressure checks, air filter changes, antifreeze, and belt and battery checks are just some of the most basic car care needs. You'll need to figure out who's taking care of all these things for each car. If your partner can do so, great—if not, you'll need to take a more active role than you may have before if your previous partner handled the car servicing.

Cars and Teens

Perhaps one of your teenagers already has a vehicle of his or her own. Lucky you! Or one teen may be becoming really interested in cars for the usual reasons. Either way, here are some suggestions for overseeing issues with a teen's car:

- Familiarize your teenagers with the above-mentioned car-care needs.
- Familiarize each teenage driver and/or car owner about the ongoing costs of car operation, including gas, servicing, repairs, and insurance, whether they have a car of their own or simply drive one of yours.
- Ask them to help pay for insurance. Insurance becomes expensive when teens are on the policy.

You or your partner will need to mentor teens as they learn to drive—yet another opportunity for bonding. Often, stepdads share lots of common ground with their protégés here. Cars can, indeed, be a vehicle of communication. (Pun intended.)

Monitoring Homework

We briefly discussed the whole concept of school achievement and homework in Chapter 8. Because it's a huge issue that often affects your relationship with the child, your husband, and the whole family at times, we'll go into more depth here.

The word "homework" can evoke the same kind of fear and horror with parents as it does with children. Some parents, however, might be grateful when the kids have homework so they have some time to get other things done. After you say, "Go upstairs and do your homework," do you think, "Ahhhhh. Finally, some quality time for me and my husband!"?

Think again. With test scores in question and schools under the gun with federal legislation regarding achievement levels, expectations for your kids' schoolwork are higher than ever. Thus, homework demands are becoming greater and more challenging for many students. If you have independent children or stepchildren who take ownership and responsibility for their homework and school-related demands, homework probably isn't an issue. But for the rest of you, monitoring and helping with homework can be upsetting for both of you.

We have heard and experienced with many parents the nightmarish cyclical dilemma that their evenings can become. You are harping about homework and school responsibilities, and the child is procrastinating and crying that they don't "get it" and "it's too hard," and you end up doing half (or all) of it for them just to get it done. You're frustrated and they're frustrated. You are upset when they don't understand the concept after you've explained it more than once and one or both of you is in, or close to, tears. They are upset because, "That's not the way Mrs. So-and-So does it!"

Foster Independence

Clearly, the situation becomes overwhelming and unproductive very quickly. Instead of descending into the same old fight, work toward a goal of fostering independence. Your goal is to be supportive while making your children as academically independent as possible. You and your partner help build and develop the child's skills while intending to have the child eventually make it on her own.

Though it can be frustrating and time-consuming, you must lend support to children who have difficulty, for whatever reason, with school-related responsibilities. But if you're not careful, this relationship can dominate your evenings and make you dread the whole homework scene. The key is lending support while still fostering independence!

It's difficult when your children are struggling *not* to charge in and take over the task. "Helping" can easily become "doing." But don't despair. We'll show you how to work together to establish a good homework routine, assist without "enabling," and avoid the homework hassle every night. Remember, you want to empower your children and help them become independent thinkers and problem-solvers. That will not happen if you do everything for them. You also need to let them know that you *are* here to help and support. We know this sounds like an impossible mission, and how do you figure out where to draw the line?

The "What Have You Tried?" Method

Here's one short and simple method that we have found works for many families. When your child whines, "I don't get this," ask him, "What have you tried?" Don't just jump right in and answer the question or help him figure it out until he can share with you what he has done on his own to resolve the problem. This technique, at the very least, expects the child to be resourceful enough to know he has to have some legitimate response that shows you he has attempted at least two (for example) different strategies for problem solving. Kids are taught very effective problem-solving strategies in school and they need to utilize them independently at home as well.

Families who find this strategy successful say that "Ask mom or dad," becomes last on the list of strategies their child uses to solve a task. Eventually your children may just figure out how to become good problem-solvers and investigate different resources to find the answers on their own. You can hope!

A CHECKLIST FOR HOMEWORK SUCCESS

- Develop a plan and get help from the school
- Stick to a consistent time and place for doing homework

- Don't give in to whining or guilt
- Foster independence
- Plan your next vacation

Working with the School

It *is* your responsibility as a parent, step or otherwise, to lend support and monitor your child's homework and whether or not it's getting done and turned in. With some children you don't have to give it a second thought, and with others you may not be aware there's a problem until the school calls you for a special conference. We can't stress enough the importance of working with your child's teacher and the school. If you have a child with special academic needs, you and the school need to work together to figure out the best academic plan for your child's success. Historically, parents do not make good teachers. You're their parent first and do not assume the role of evening teacher. Let the experts advise you.

School Functions: Who Goes?

When possible, both of you should attend school functions, fundraisers, programs, and, most importantly, parent-teacher conferences. If he attends alone because you don't want to encounter the biological mom there, you aren't giving the child, the teacher, and the school a good impression. You are a team, and you need to be presenting that approach regarding school and your role as a "mom," which are both so critical in a child's life. If you absolutely can't be in the same room with your husband's ex, or she refuses to attend if you're there, maybe you can schedule two separate conferences with the child's teacher. But come on—you're the adult. Expecting teachers to schedule additional conferences because one or the other of you can't act like one is really unfair to the teacher. It is important that you hear the same things and not take the chance of two different sessions yielding two totally diverse interpretations.

Staying close to, and involved in, the children's school life is critical in ensuring their success and your connectedness to them. Just as with the parent-teacher conferences, expect that the biological mother will probably also be there, and don't feel insecure or threatened by that. So much of a child's life is centered around school—it's important that you all show an appropriate level of involvement. Here are some other tips:

- Stay on top of events going on in the children's academic life, and know their school achievement levels.
- Communicate often and as needed with the children's teachers. Some teachers will even send you daily e-mails, which is a good way to communicate regarding behavior problems or academic issues or concerns. Just remember that your stepchild is only one of many for his or her teacher, and be reasonable about how you use the teacher's time.
- Sign up for as many things as your schedule allows. Volunteer and offer to attend special functions and events. Go watch their games and performances. We know you both can't always attend, but at least one of you needs to be there every time you can. Does it cut into your schedule? Of course it does, but the contribution of your time and interest in your stepchildren's school life is essential. They want so much for you to be interested in what they're doing at school, even if they don't always say it.

Staying involved in the school community as the children grow older is one of the best ways you have to monitor their success, know what's going on in their lives, and help them avoid the pitfalls that all children face at one time or another.

Transporting the Kids

Get ready for a different lifestyle if you don't have children yourself. Here's the part where you trade the little red sports car for the family van. (Really, some vans are pretty plush—and so versatile!) For those of you who have already been the quintessential taxi mom, little will change, except with his kids, you might need a bigger van.

The Nuisances . . . and the Upside

What a merging family means is more miles on the road. Although the prices go up and down, gasoline will eat a chunk of your monthly budget no matter what it costs. It also means that you personally will be stretched in more directions than you might have anticipated. You may literally be transporting kids almost every night of the week. Wear and tear on the vehicle? What about wear and tear on you? Many moms and dads shake their heads in bewilderment over this issue—but almost always with pride. Most genuinely enjoy being involved and reliving their childhood. It's fun to root for a team or watch a performance, especially if one of your children is playing or acting. (We know of grandparents who enjoy it, too.) Maybe one or both of you might be coaching a team as well.

What a healthy outlet for boundless energy! Sports teach lifelong skills and teamwork, and they help keep kids fit and in good physical condition. Likewise for theater, music lessons, and other extracurricular activities. Many kids find a wholesome expression that they otherwise would not have known. They may discover abilities they were previously unaware of. Convinced yet? We hope so. All those practices, rehearsals, and meetings are important, so you'll have to grin and bear it.

Who Does the Transporting?

Yes, there is the issue of who transports them. Depending on the size of the family, you may each be driving different kids to different locations. Often, one of you may not be available, so the other one picks up the slack. As with other routines, it's best to work out who's doing what beforehand with your partner. Modifying work schedules may help ensure that one or both of you is available when needed. We're sure that once you get involved, you will get hooked and will accept any necessary lifestyle modifications as part of the bargain.

More on Curfews

We talked about curfews already in Chapter 8. Why mention it again? Because it's so important. Knowing the whereabouts of each child and what they are doing at all times says that you care. It registers with kids, and they do appreciate it, even if they don't tell you that! Communication about curfews at regular intervals is a must.

A Case in Point: Working Effectively with School

Claire had two young children of her own and married a man with two children in junior high. The older child had many behavioral, as well as academic, concerns. While he wasn't a behavior problem at home, at school he was "off task," disinterested, irresponsible, and often disruptive. Claire's husband had tried grounding the boy and implementing other consequences, but nothing seemed to work. He had pretty much just accepted that unsuccessful dealings with the school were to be the norm for him as well as his son.

Claire was really committed to helping her new stepson, especially since his biological mother had died and her partner felt helpless. She tried monitoring whether his homework was done, and helping him with his lessons and school responsibilities. Before long, she learned that "I'm bored" and "I don't like this" usually meant "it's too hard."

She started working with the school guidance counselor, and they, along with his teachers, developed a behavior plan. Parents, teachers, and child each had a role to play. She took her new son to the doctor and found out that he actually was a bright child who had Attention Deficit Disorder. The school agreed to modify his requirements and give him special resource support.

Kids with ADD without hyperactivity often fall through the cracks and are misread and labeled as lazy or unmotivated. Once the child started taking medication (which he met with much resistance at first) and got into a workable routine with responsibility and support, his life took a 180-degree turn.

"Is everything perfect in our lives at home? No, but we're at a place where I never thought we would be. Brian is a different person. He even tried out and made the eighth-grade basketball team. We have great hopes for him in high school."

Author's Note

We are neither promoting nor discouraging the use of medication with children with ADD and/or ADHD. We simply report different case studies as they have been presented to us. The use of medications is particular to each child, each family, and each situation.

REFLECTIONS: KEY ISSUES IN CHAPTER 10

- Study your unique situation. List every responsibility that needs daily and weekly attention. Divide, assign duties, and conquer.

- For household repairs and lawn and gardening duties, it comes down to who has the most skill, time, and desire for each. Many of these responsibilities provide a creative outlet and a source of pride. Kids can learn invaluable skills here.

- Most often, we look to Dad for auto servicing and repair. But, be aware, there are ladies out there who are better than their male mates at this stuff.

- Monitoring homework usually gets to be the job of whoever is present and has skills in the needed area.

- Both parents should attend school functions in which their kids or stepkids are involved. It's an index of interest and caring.

- Both parents should transport the kids, based on schedules and availability.

- You and your partner should always know where your kids are and who they're with. Have them call you to check in when they are out.

Part Three

Achieving Long-Term Success

Chapter 11

Surviving Holidays, Birthdays, and Vacations

"I spent hours fixing this huge holiday feast. The kids wolfed it down, were here for an hour and a half, and then sped off to their see their biological mom. The next week I baked my stepson's birthday cake, shopped for his present, and fixed his favorite meal. Did I get a thank-you? Of course not. Then, all of them totally ignored my birthday. Next week, we leave for the family vacation. What happened to those getaways with just my guy and me? How do other people do this?"

With some thoughtful preplanning, discussion, and communication prior to the big family events, you will develop your own rituals and traditions born out of mutual consideration, concessions, and adjustment. It takes time. Remember that Rome wasn't built in a day.

Who Gets the Kids for Christmas This Year?

Is there any holiday that can trigger emotion the way that Christmas (or the winter holiday your family celebrates) does? The prep and work alone are massive. Planning for meals, inviting guests, decorating the house and tree, parties and activities, Christmas cards, school programs, and the colossal task of gift buying—the hype and expense for many has become overwhelming. Families have usually established long-standing traditions, and kids are intent on making sure it's done "the way we've always done it." And what is Christmas without Grandma? "We always go to Grandma's!"

Preparations

We hate to say it, but the majority of Christmas prep and execution typically falls on the woman. Men typically put up the outside lights and get the tree in the stand, but other than buying some gifts on the afternoon of Christmas Eve, his job is pretty much done. Not to minimize his role in any way—every situation is different—but most families depend on Mom to make it all happen. It's hard enough when you're *not* in a stepfamily to get through it. Now add another person, his kids, and his "ex" and the task becomes even more daunting.

You probably have your own rituals that you and your kids have followed forever. Both you and your partner may even have worked out an equitable exchange with your exes to share the kids over the holidays. (Or your choices may be limited if the court has decided "who goes where.") Now you're in a new family and both sets of kids want everything to be the way it always has been. You just want to spend Christmas morning with your own immediate family (including your stepkids), celebrating together. You might even want to fit in a few poignant moments alone with your husband (ha!). You also have to consider your husband's parents, his siblings, cousins, and an undetermined number of friends. You may dread the holiday long before Halloween arrives and wish you could skip the whole event. Or maybe Christmas has always been your favorite holiday in spite of the variables you can't control, and you're determined to make it a huge success and keep everybody happy. Is your head spinning yet?

Making It Work

You *can* get through it and save your sanity as well. As with everything, you and your husband need to decide where the kids will be long before the big event. Here are some things for the two of you to consider:

- Can you celebrate with someone on a different day? Christmas doesn't always have to be on December 25. You can get together with extended family anytime during the holidays.
- How much will you spend on gifts? Decide on a budget and stick to it. Does everything have to be equitable? Pretty much.
- Where will you be on the most important two days? Figure out where you will be on Christmas Eve and Christmas Day and with whom.

The important thing is that you agree and decide together. Patience and compromise will go a long way in making the season pleasant. You may have to accept a different way of doing things, but that's part of having a successful marriage with stepkids. Do you have to forego everything you want? Of course not, but flexibility is the key, and if you really want the season to be special for you as a new family unit, you can do it!

Involve the Kids

Of course, you need to ask the kids how they would like to spend the holiday. Do they have the last word? No, but you absolutely need to consider their feelings when you are planning.

Learn to delegate responsibilities throughout the season and make everyone's contribution in the whole event known. Kids can help decorate, water the tree, and maybe even wrap gifts. Also, help them understand what's important about the season. If they're angry because they've always had a live blue spruce and now you have an artificial tree, talk in age-appropriate ways about how blending a family means starting new traditions. Does it matter if the tree isn't perfect and the tinsel isn't hung exactly as you would like? You already know the answer. Be sure the kids know it too.

See the Bigger Picture

Someday, it will be just the two of you. Look ahead and remember that before you know it, the kids will grow up and have their own families, including in-laws, and you'll be wondering where the two of you fit in.

In spite of the work and possible ulcer, we can't think of anything better than to have your home be the *welcome* gathering place where everyone can experience joy and good tidings. What a great legacy to leave your kids, and it's something they will always remember.

If you're especially frustrated, remember that January is right around the corner.

School's Out and They're All Going to Be Here

"There's nothing to do here!"

"Johnny's mom and dad are gone, so can I go over to his house?"

Everybody loves summer, right? Anyone who's experienced a long summer with bored kids understands the parents who say, "I can't wait until school starts." Summer can be a long dry spell for kids away from their school friends, and there is nothing worse than hearing "I'm boooored" on the second week of vacation. And there is nothing worse for their minds and bodies than sitting around watching TV, playing video games, hanging out on the Internet (watch this one especially closely), or sending 100 text messages a day. Keeping kids active and constructive over the summer months can take a lot of planning on your part, but it's essential to their well-being as well as a successful start to the next school year. Kids lose a lot of information over the summer when their minds are not being challenged in the same way as during the school year.

Plan Ahead

If you work outside the home, you obviously have to make child care arrangements for the kids while you are at work. Camps and day cares fill up quickly, so be sure you determine who's going where sometime in the spring.

If you're home with the kids over the summer, there are many great activities that you can plan for them to minimize idle time. (Yes, they need *some* down time, but too much is unhealthy and counterproductive.) Here are some universal ideas for all ages:

- Visit the library to keep them involved with books.
- Plan trips to the zoo.
- Have the kids pack a lunch for a picnic in the park.
- Consider summer camps for a week or two. If your funds are limited, you can be creative and do things together where cost is minimal.
- Give them extra chores since they have extra time on their hands!

- Help your teens find a job.
- Arrange for the kids to visit their friends.

Of course, some of the summer will likely be spent with the other biological parent. You need to plan for that as well—when exactly is the visit happening, who's driving/picking up, who is paying for what.

Since everyone is going in different directions and out of school routines, the summer may call for a master schedule or some kind of calendar. The summer can be a great time for you to bond and experience fun activities together, but you have to be organized and not expect things to take care of themselves. If you have a willy-nilly approach, be prepared for "What can I do?" on day two. Don't try, "Clean your room," or you'll just hear, "I don't mean *work!*" Sound familiar? Be proactive and plan ahead. You will avoid frustration for them and yourselves if you have a plan for the family and set guidelines on which you and your husband can agree.

Sleepovers

Every child should have an opportunity to spend the night at a friend's house or have a friend stay over at your house. It's a part of growing up that every child should experience. The situation gets sticky when you don't like your kids' friends.

Tips for Handling Sleepovers

Sleepovers are usually a blast for the kids and a headache for parents. Here are some ways to minimize the damage:

- Remember that it's your house, so set some expectations for behavior in advance.

- When scheduling sleepovers, set limits as to how often. Every weekend is a little excessive. You need to decide what you are comfortable with.
- Don't be too strict. Give kids some extra time to stay up later at night, but tell them when you say "lights out," it needs to happen.
- Consider that when teens have a friend over, they'll probably be up much later and want to sleep most of the next day. If that's okay with you, there's no problem. If it isn't okay, make that clear beforehand.
- Remind kids of all ages that under no circumstances should they be allowed to leave the house and roam the neighborhood after you're asleep.
- Remember that you are responsible for what happens to your kids and their friends while they're under your roof, so know what's going on.

The bottom line: You want your kids to feel comfortable inviting their friends to your home. It's a good reward for positive behavior on their part. It's also a nice way to encourage friendships that you think are healthy and positive. But don't feel goaded into doing it constantly if you are uncomfortable with it.

Sonya told us that she and her husband only had visitation with his kids every other weekend. That amounts to only four nights a month, and "Can I bring a friend to spend the night?" was the first thing they always heard. With limited time together, they preferred to have the kids alone, but knew they would have to compromise and allow occasional overnights. Each of the two girls got to ask a friend to spend the night only once a month, and Sonya and her husband tried to explain their reasoning. Remember that things like sleepovers with friends come in phases, and this is probably not going to last forever.

Know as well that it's a compliment when your kids and stepkids ask if they can invite someone to dinner or to stay overnight. It means they feel good about where they are and want to share it with others. If they always want to stay elsewhere and never invite anyone to your home, step back and evaluate the reason.

That Friend You Don't Like

If there is someone you don't particularly care for, discourage the friendship discreetly, but remember that can backfire—the child may only want to see the friend *more* if you forbid it. And look at it this way—wouldn't you rather have that friend at your house where you can monitor what goes on?

"On My Birthday, I Want to Be with My Real Mom"

Think of birthdays as mini-Christmases. While the expense and preparation are not the same, logistical problems are still there as far as what, when, where, and who.

Your husband may have a visitation arrangement with his children's mother. If your stepkids live with their mom, those timing considerations are probably already decided as well. As with Christmas, you do *not* have to celebrate the event on the actual day. Be flexible and allow the kids some latitude in decision making for how and where they want to spend their day.

Spend Within Your Limits

If you're planning a party, do so within your means, and don't be guilt-tripped into doing more or spending more than you are able. If the kids come home from Mom's with expensive toys and the latest electronic gadgets, be gracious and say how happy you are that they like their gifts from Mom. (If they live with you, she may be experiencing some guilt at not having her children full-time.) Never make spending a competition between you and the other biological parents. So many people fall into this trap and get into a financial mess because of it. Do what you can, don't feel guilty, and that's all there is. You can make birthdays a lot of fun without a lot of expense.

Oh, You Have a Birthday Too?

Now how do you respond when they don't remember or recognize your birthday at all? Know that this is common, particularly in the beginning. The kids are all wrapped up in adjusting to the new routine. Please be understanding. You're the grownup.

The (Dreaded) Family Vacation

Trying to plan a family vacation where everyone has a good time can be a daunting task. Someone only likes the beach and someone else hates it. You can plan a trip to Florida, and it rains every day. You go to a theme park, and the cost is staggering, the line is a mile long, it's $5 for a hot dog, and it's 95 degrees. It's no wonder you might need a week off to recover from a vacation. Despite the problems, family vacations can be the best time for bonding and really getting to know each other. (Of course, there is the chance that can work in the reverse and no one's speaking when it's over.)

Bringing Friends

If you are contemplating a family vacation that involves traveling, planning is the key. Don't just take off and let the trip work itself out. That doesn't work with kids, especially teenagers who didn't want to leave their friends anyway.

Be prepared to either bring an extra person along (kids are notorious for asking, "Can I bring a friend?") or to tell kids that it's a family-only trip. You have to decide whether it's in the budget or counterproductive to your family time. Keep in mind, also, that life might be more harmonious if the kids do have a friend along. Rotate through the family in deciding who can invite whom.

Let the Kids Have Their Say

Let the kids have input as to where they would like to go and what they would like to do. After all, it is supposed to be fun for all of you. Maybe the kids have always gone to the same place every year and don't want to change. Be flexible. (Have we mentioned that before?) You might have to "gut it up" and try their location at least once. You might discover that you really like their choice. That said, there is certainly something special about creating your own new traditions with this new family. Let everyone have some input and express an opinion.

A Case in Point: Merry Christmas

Kate had always loved Christmas; it was her favorite holiday. Her new husband's two kids had lived alone with him for some time, and they had their own way of doing things. They wanted a huge real tree, and they had their own decorations they had used for years. Kate had things, as well, that had been in her family for a long time. She never realized how much conflict and resentment could come from just decorating a tree!

The kids always went to their grandmother's for dinner and gifts on Christmas Eve and then to Grandma's church service. Kate and her boys always went to her mother's on Christmas Eve and to mass at her own church. No one wanted to compromise and change what they had always done. So, on their first Christmas Eve together, Kate and her husband, Dave, each went their own way with their own kids. So much for a first Christmas together as a family.

Christmas Day wasn't much better when the family came together to open gifts in the morning. As soon as the gifts were opened, Dave's son and daughter left to go to their aunt's and never touched the Christmas brunch that Kate had painstakingly prepared. She and Dave blamed each other for this unsuccessful first holiday. Each was angry at the other, as well as the kids, and Kate wondered if she had made a huge mistake in getting involved with this family.

They headed to counseling rather than throw in the towel. An outside mediator helped them determine which things were really important in their family and to the two of them. Once they were able to put their anger aside and put things into perspective, they realized that each had a responsibility in bringing about change in tradition without compromising the meaning of the holiday.

"I was dreading our second Christmas, but Dave and I made a pact that we were going to stick together in creating new family traditions and still let the kids do the things that had become so important to them. Our parents had to appreciate that changes were in order as well. I had to give in on a lot of things, but once I realized that our own rituals would evolve and Dave and I were on the same page, I was able to do it without being furious."

REFLECTIONS: KEY ISSUES IN CHAPTER 11

- Planning special days and holidays for newly blended families requires much planning and cooperation with the kids and ex-spouses.

- Do's and don'ts need to be clear when the kid's friends stay over.

- Treat birthdays as mini-holidays in terms of when and with whom the kids spend time.

- Family vacations can be bonding and great fun, but also very stressful without planning.

Chapter 12

Religion and Culture

Don't skip this chapter just because you and your new husband are both white Anglo-Saxon Protestants and were reared in the same city, and you believe you have no cultural, religious, or spiritual differences. Dr. Neil Clark Warren, founder of eHarmony.com, researched twenty-nine dimensions of human characteristics on which couples may differ, including good character, spirituality, family background, intellect, sense of humor, sexual passion, industriousness, curiosity, sociability, dominance versus submission, and more. Consider also such variables as nationality, language, age, race, religion, and the myriad combinations these differences generate. Let's face it: We're all different. These differences can be highly challenging as well as enriching and broadening—if you're open to new views and behavior.

Cultural Differences

Nationality and race often bring with them multiple differences in language, customs, dress, attitudes toward childrearing, food preferences, and more. Let's look at some examples of each.

Language

Beverly went on a couple of dates with a distinguished-looking Asian-American man. Although he was professionally successful, the gentleman had not yet mastered the English language. As it turned out, he had not yet integrated well into American culture either and had essentially lived and worked almost wholly within the Asian subsector of his city. Beverly remarked, "I felt drained after each outing. It was such a strain to try to understand what he was saying. I don't think he had truly tried to integrate himself into the outside world yet."

Issues like the above can involve stepchildren as well. A key element, we believe, is the person's intent and willingness to be a better communicator. If your partner or his kids speak a different language, all parties should strive toward becoming at least conversant, if not fluent, in each other's primary language. It can be a fun, bonding, and broadening experience. Best of all, it is a "together" family exercise. The better you communicate with each other, the more deeply you understand each other, and the easier it is to love each other. Learning a new language involves learning about the culture in which it is spoken as well.

Food Preferences

New stepmom Shikira cooked an elaborate Japanese dinner for her Caucasian stepson. He took one look and announced, "I'm not eating this." Shikira was crushed, not realizing that his objection was not to the food or to her, but rather an unresolved resentment for having had his life disrupted.

You can avoid this situation by simply asking preferences before spending all day in the kitchen preparing five-course meals. When you're ready to introduce the kids to one of your culture's special dishes, do so gradually and casually. For example, one night make it just for you and your partner. The kids can watch you and him relishing the dish, and you may stimulate their curiosity. Or ask the children to help you prepare it.

Do Unto Others

If your new family has a particular dish you're unfamiliar with, act like an adult, show genuine interest in the recipe, and give it a shot.

Childrearing Practices

Childrearing attitudes vary greatly across cultures—even by families from different regions of the same country. In the southern United States, for example, many parents still foster the use of *Mister, Sir,* and *Ma'am* when addressing adults. In other cultures, seeing children rather than hearing them is the overriding philosophy. Formality versus informality is frequently a distinguishing issue.

Resolving variances in child-rearing practices and expectations requires cooperation and compromise between stepmom and new husband. We can't stress enough to speak with your partner early on about these issues, as they're unlikely to be something you can change. If your mate genuinely acts in the best interests of your children, good things happen.

Modes of Dress

Men and women are frequently attracted to each other partially based on what the other is wearing. Cultural differences can be an attractive plus in these cases if you like your partner's unique clothes.

But opposites and differences can turn problematic, such as the fashion and dress preferences of children and adults. Please be aware of these issues and know that they can incubate and inflame. If you need to change someone's dress for a legitimate reason, tread lightly. Reinforcing more tasteful and modest fashions is generally more effective than criticizing overly bold displays.

Age

Differences in ages can take on many variations in a stepfamily, especially one filled with kids. There's your age and his age, and your kids' ages, plus how close in age you are to his kids, and vice versa. Let's take a look at each.

His Kids and Your Kids

Wide disparities in age between your kids and his kids can be both potentially beneficial and problematic. If the age differences are really wide, it can hamper bonding and limit some activities you can do as a group. For example, six-year-old Johnny may idealize his sixteen-year-old stepbrother, but the latter may be engrossed in his teenage peer group and not want to bother with the youngster. On the other hand, some teenage siblings take on a protective stance to younger stepsibs and enjoy teaching them certain skills.

If the kids are close in age, again, you'll find positives and negatives. If they're young, they may play together easily. As they get older, though, realize that stepchildren of similar age, having no blood relationship, can and do become romantically involved. One former stepmom pointed out that her former stepdaughter is now her daughter-in-law and that the marriage is going well. It does stand to reason that adults who are attracted to each other may have children with biological and acquired qualities that encourage attraction as well.

You and His Kids

Special challenges face stepmoms much older than or very close in age to their stepchildren. Older stepmoms may be viewed as out of touch with teenage slang, activities, and music preferences. Younger stepmoms may come to be viewed more as a buddy or a friend rather than one who must act with authority on occasion. And don't forget that teenage stepsons can and do become attracted to younger stepmoms.

How to Handle the Age Differences

You and your partner need to be aware of the pros and cons of the ages you're dealing with. If you sense problems due to your age, you may need to modify your behavior and carefully monitor that of your children. For example, choose some activities that both a six-year-old and a teen can enjoy together, like going to a ballgame, the library, or watching certain movies. Some sixteen-year-olds enjoy teaching and mentoring younger kids in athletics and other skills.

If Your Stepson Is Attracted to You

If you're even close to your stepson's age, you may find yourself in an awkward situation where he becomes attracted to you. In this case, you'll need to avoid vulnerable situations. If you sense that your teenage stepson is attracted to you, think about these cures:

1. Do not wear revealing clothing when he is in your home.
2. Remember that he may misperceive simple gestures of affection, so be careful about using them. If the situation is serious enough, stop the gestures altogether for a time.
3. Help him with dating strategies for girls his own age.
4. Inform his father of what you are feeling. Maybe a father-son talk is in order here. Dad should explain that the attraction is inappropriate but express his love for his son at the same time.

Socioeconomic Background

If you and your partner come from very different financial situations, you will probably find that your lifestyles are quite different. If your partner's divorce caused him to lose some of his wealth, for example, his kids might miss the expensive things they're used to. Designer handbags, the latest in expensive electronics, and expensive prom gowns may now be for window shopping only. Stepkids who are accustomed to the "good life" may mistakenly hold you responsible for newfound limitations.

Belt-tightening is not a comfortable exercise for anyone. Children may become confused, frustrated, and resentful. Parents may feel guilty and experience regret. A saving grace may lie in providing kids with choices such as, "We can't go to Florida *and* take a cruise this year. Which would you like to do?" At any rate, your partner and his ex-wife should tell the kids about the reasons for the new economics in a timely, nonblaming manner. You should not be framed as the villain, whatever the circumstances. If you hear the kids saying it's one parent's fault or the other's, objectively present the situation without vilifying anyone's character.

Religious and Spiritual Differences

If you and your partner have different religious or spiritual convictions, you may already know the difficulties it can cause in a relationship. Factor in his kids (and yours) and things get even more complicated. Let's look at some of the factors at play in this sticky scenario.

We're Not the Same Religion

Consider the possibilities. You might find yourself in a family with several varying denominational views. All of you might find it fascinating to discuss and debate such different points of view with no one becoming offended. Or some may refuse to talk of their beliefs and prefer to be more secretive about them. Some may be intrigued by the origin of the various sects, while others could care less. Clearly, wide diversities exist, and parents and children alike will hold on to them fiercely. Your reactions may range from, "That's their business," to "Oh my gosh, I need to save these people."

Knowing in advance that your new husband and children have values, religious or otherwise, that vary from yours allows you an up-front opportunity to develop a system with which everyone can live. Perhaps it involves attending different churches or both of you visiting the other's church from time to time. What about stepchildren who do not wish to attend church at all? What if they do and you do not? These questions are best settled early on. There are no "right" answers we can give you—the key is to take everyone's views seriously and teach and practice tolerance on all levels.

Considering the Kids' Biological Parents' Wishes

Religious preferences and church attendance can be a sensitive issue to both biological and stepparents. Former stepmom Rachel noted that many such potential problems are averted by divorce-decree stipulations. Even if that's the case, you might find that the devil is in the details: Who's taking the kids to church? Should they participate in religious education or activities? What if you are lax about motivating children and stepchildren to attend?

These challenges aside, you need to honor the kids' biological parents' mandates. Although it remains the father's primary responsibility, he will appreciate it if you help facilitate the biological mom's wishes for her children.

Occasionally, biological parents have neither denominational nor church-attendance preferences for their children. In this case, you could consider extending an invitation to attend your church with you. Get the consent of both biological parents before proceeding. Children may be interested in going with you to spend time with someone who cares, for the social aspects of church life, or to sincerely explore the particular beliefs your religion holds.

Understanding Why You're Different

When asked if differences in religious beliefs could be a problem, Sandy summarized the general stepmom stance, saying, "Yes, it can be a problem if you're dogmatic." Certain stepmoms do feel disturbed by beliefs that seem, or in fact are, in direct opposition to their own. Keep in mind that our constitutional forefathers ensured that Americans would enjoy freedom of religion. Freedom of religion means that you are free to believe as you wish, while at the same time you are obliged to allow others the same privilege.

Consider the particular path or series of circumstances that brought you to your current personal belief system. You may have had significant experiences that were paramount in your development. Now understand that your partner and his children were simply raised on a different path. They have experienced different environments, parents, and models. They too may have undergone experiences that nourished their thinking. Therefore, they may not embrace the viewpoints you hold.

Presenting—Not Imposing—Values and Beliefs

There are big differences between presenting and imposing values and beliefs. *Presenting* your beliefs involves explaining their rationale and logic. Your explanation should illustrate how you developed your position and why it makes sense to you. *Imposing* a belief assumes that you want to make others believe as you do. Imposition implies a certain pressure to take your approach, either by means of suggested rewards or punishment, however subtly offered.

While it is acceptable to present or explain dogma to your new family, it is definitely not okay to impose your belief patterns on others, whatever their age. In the end, it is up to the child to either accept or refuse to incorporate the particular values in question. While states differ as to exact age, when the children grow up they will decide for themselves what values they choose to embrace.

When all is said and done, what matters most is whether you have walked the talk—that is, whether you behave the way you say you believe.

Spiritual but Not Religious?

Several recent surveys have shown a progressive increase in those declaring that they are "spiritual" as opposed to "religious." For our purposes, we define religion as "a set of beliefs, values, and practices based on the teachings of a spiritual leader," per the American Heritage Dictionary. This generally assumes an adherence to an organized denomination and membership therein. By contrast, many of our stepmoms view spirituality as a more personal search for one's own path and/or relationship with God, a deity, or higher power, rather than following the principles of a given religion or denomination. The benefits of a spiritual stance are greater freedom of belief and behavior, in that it allows for a personal search, as opposed to resigning oneself to an already organized system. Critics of the spiritual approach suggest that it is ever-changing, difficult to define, and provides adherents with readymade excuses to do whatever they wish.

If your stepkids follow a spiritual path and you don't, they might be more accepting of you because they respect those who are members of a given religion. On the other hand, if they follow a given religion and you're the spiritual one, they might have difficulty understanding the more abstract spiritual approach. Obviously, you can see the potential discomfort with these contrasting approaches.

The key is to adopt a mindset of openness. You'll learn more, show that you genuinely care about others' interests, and broaden your horizons.

What's This New Age Stuff about, Anyway?

The terms New Age, occult, and paranormal have become especially popularized by television, film, and publishing industries in recent years. The American Heritage Dictionary provides the following definitions for each:

New Age: Of, or relating to, a complex of spiritual and consciousness-raising movements of the 1980s, including belief in spiritualism, reincarnation, and holistic approaches to health and ecology.

Occult: Of, relating to, or dealing with supernatural influences, agencies, or phenomena.

Paranormal: Beyond the range of normal or scientific explanation.

Wicca: A polytheistic Neo-Pagan nature religion inspired by various pre-Christian western European beliefs, whose central deity is a mother goddess and which includes the use of herbal magic and benign witchcraft.

We've found that people run the gamut from believing almost every "paranormal" story they hear to those who believe none of it. More people believe in certain of the above phenomena than they will openly admit.

Why do you need to know about these things? As we said, they've grown in popularity recently, and you may find that your stepchildren are interested in spell casting or meditation. Again, keep an open mind. If your son or stepson announces that he is now a Wiccan or a Druid, your best approach is to thoroughly research that particular sect. You then have an avenue of communication and can bring informed reasoning into play when discussing his choice.

A Case in Point:
Finding a Spiritual Common Ground

When Sarah and Matt decided to marry, they recognized that their religious backgrounds and differences would be a challenge. Sarah was raised in a traditional Jewish household steeped in tradition. She was bringing up her son in the same manner. Matt and his two children were Catholic, and Matt was working to obtain an annulment and struggled with his "divorced" status. They loved each other and thought somehow they would be able to blend together and recognize and celebrate both faiths. They were married in a civil ceremony with both parties thinking they would have their marriage blessed at a later date by their respective church and temple.

Initially, they both attended their own places of worship with their children and went their separate ways on those days. As couples often do when they're struggling to form their new family and cement their relationship amid different religions, they each stopped going to religious services altogether. They tried instead to bond closer together as a family, but each of them silently felt the loss of such an important component in their lives and the lives of their children. It began to create a wedge between the two of them as each felt they were "giving up" a way of life that had been ingrained in their spiritual formation.

Before disaster overwhelmed the new family completely, Matt and Sarah sought the help and intervention of their priest and rabbi. Matt's priest was helping him to work through his annulment and had become quite vested in the success of his new marriage. Through outside intervention and the help of these spiritual professionals, the couple was able to find a commonality in their beliefs and practices. They both recognized the Old Testament and the Ten Commandments, and they had a profound belief in God. On this foundation, they began to build a renewed sense of spiritual life and commitment to each other. Is it perfect and ideal? No. But they now recognize both faiths and celebrate the special occasions of each. Learning about the faith of their partners has brought about a deeper connection to their own.

REFLECTIONS: KEY ISSUES IN CHAPTER 12

- Differences in nationality, ethnicity, and race can provide both challenges and enrichment.

- Variances in food preferences, child-rearing practices, modes of dress, age, and socioeconomic background can be seen as stressful (if not approached with openness) or as an opportunity for growth (if approached with respect).

- You need to honor the religious preferences of the kids' biological parents.

- An open mind is the best tool in coping with religious differences.

- When dealing with New Age or Wiccan religions, research the element in question to gain an informed position.

Chapter 13

(Step)Money Matters

How the money moves is often one of the most potent deal breakers in subsequent marriages. Stepkids can compound this times ten. First, who pays for the basics? Did you touch on this before saying "I do"? Who pays for his kids' and your kids' "special" expenses, such as those $200 sneakers and $500 prom dresses? This can be tricky stuff. Veteran stepmoms provide solutions to some of these emotionally charged issues.

It is important to look well beyond the present situation and thoroughly examine your future financial plans and structure, which include health benefits, 401(k)s, and retirement accounts. Set up a household budget, but be prepared for unforeseen expenses that can tap into your financial security. Be certain to have a well-developed sketch that defines the financial responsibilities of each party and takes into account all sources of income.

Family Income: Who Works?

Before you met your partner, chances are you were employed somewhere (unless you are independently wealthy). You might have an amazing career that fulfills you financially as well as in every other way. People work for a variety of reasons, and money is usually only part of the reason. You may have no intention, desire, or inclination to leave your profession, or you may be in a position you despise and would love nothing more than to be a stay-at-home mom who does not work outside the home. (Note, that we said "outside the home" as there isn't a mom we've met anywhere who "doesn't work.")

Whatever the situation you face, come to a mutual understanding and agreement about each of your jobs. Juggling a career and being either a full-time or weekend-only mom is a huge challenge. Your schedule is pulled in a thousand different ways, and somehow the crux of getting to work, running the home, and transporting and meeting the kids' needs falls *primarily* on you. (We don't mean to offend any of the modern-day dads who seem to do it all as well, but we're just being realistic. We also recognize that there are stay-at-home dads who also take on those responsibilities.)

As with most things, you and your partner need to pre-plan before you get married and determine, as we referenced in Chapter 3, what your financial needs will be. Obviously you can't foresee any future calamities, but you can have the master plan. This doesn't mean that it is written in stone; financial needs do change. Here are some possible scenarios:

- **You both work:** If you are both employed, you can both share, to some degree, in the financial responsibilities of running the home.
- **He works and you stay home:** Maybe he objects to you working outside the home and really wants you to be at home with the kids. If his finances can support that, and that is what you want, great. There is much peace of

mind that comes with staying home with little ones, as long as you aren't sacrificing a huge chunk of income to do so. If your job (and it is a job) is working in the home only, we hope you both agree that it is a most equitable contribution to the family.

- **You work and he stays home:** As we said, we know of dads who stay home with the children while the wife works.

When trying to develop an equitable plan, take into account how much income you each have from all sources. If one of you isn't working outside the home, does he or she have other monetary input such as child support or investment dividends? If only one of you is employed outside the home, then obviously the majority of the financial responsibility is that person's.

The person who's not working needn't feel left out of the financial picture altogether. For example, if you're home, you could manage the bank accounts, pay the bills, and file your taxes. Whatever you decide, make sure to delve thoroughly into the overall financial structure of your home and the needs of your family as early as you can in your relationship. Yes, things change as life goes on, but it's easier to manage the ups and downs if you have a master plan in place.

Joint or Separate Accounts?

We were amazed at how all-consuming the question of "names on the accounts" could be. If you and your partner are having a disagreement about this issue, you're not alone. Some would not even consider creating a joint account, while others thought that separate accounts actually meant that a problem existed in the marriage and was an indicator that a true union didn't exist.

No matter how in love you are with someone, if things aren't equitable at the end of the day, one or both of you may feel resentment. You have to take into account how much each of you brings into the marriage to begin with, along with how much each of you earns on a regular basis. Some men have absolutely no problem turning their paycheck over to their wife to disperse among the family's needs and responsibilities. If that's the case, a joint account might work for you.

You need to feel comfortable with the account arrangements, and that's the bottom line. Whether you decide to delegate specific financial responsibilities or throw everything into one pot, you each need to feel satisfied that the order of business is *fair* to both of you. Here are some pros and cons to each:

1. **Joint accounts:** These work well for those who have decided that the money can funnel into a single pool that both partners can access whenever they need to.
2. **Separate accounts:** Separate checking accounts save a lot of confusion and help keep things accurate as far as who spent what.
3. **A combination of both:** You can also consider separate savings accounts and a joint checking account that you use just for paying bills.

Keep Things Going Smoothly

No matter what kind of accounts you have, follow these tips to keep your financial life as stress-free as possible:

- Maintain accurate records if you are both writing checks and debits out of the same account.
- Make sure that each of you feels that you have your own money and don't have to account for every dime you spend at the salon, the coffee shop, or the pro shop.

- Discuss any major expenses before making them. Set an agreed-upon amount, such as anything over $200 merits discussion.
- Don't forget to take a look into the future when it will just be the two of you. Have you saved enough for retirement?
- Consider seeking the advice of a financial professional to sort out the details of your money matters. It could be a most worthwhile investment for compatibility and peace of mind.

If one or the other of you is wealthy, the issue of money and how much might never be a worry or a concern. Unfortunately, that's most likely *not* the case in the majority of families. In today's economy with the rising cost of living, finances need to get a huge chunk of your attention prior to, as well as after, the wedding.

Who Pays for What?

Needless to say, you'll have to organize where the money comes from to pay all of the bills and obligations both of you have. We'll say it again: talk about it beforehand so you can be aware of any potential disagreements and determine a mutually acceptable solution. Following are some major categories of expenses you'll likely have and how to deal with each.

Household Bills

Once you establish a general household budget, you can decide how you will manage the bill paying. Splitting the bills and assigning some to each parent might work, but it might cause a lot of confusion. If you each contribute to a joint checking account according to your income, keep a ledger or use a computer program to keep accurate records of household expenses. Decide what is *considered* a household expense: food, utilities, insurance, mortgage payments, phone(s), minor repairs, newspapers, and other miscellaneous bills fall into this category. If something unexpected pops up, you need to decide where it falls in the "who pays" category. Of course if you're throwing everything you make into one joint-account pot, the payment responsibility is never in question.

Automobile

Whether you take care of your own car payments and insurance costs depends, again, upon how you set up your finances. We found that many women, while the husband assumed the responsibility for the majority of the household expenses, did take care of their own automobile costs. Also, a money-saving tip: insurance for more than one vehicle in a family usually affords you a discount, so take advantage and get the family's cars onto one policy.

The Kids' Personal Stuff

Oh, boy. This might seem like a minor issue, but it can become a major dilemma when trying to decide what's fair and equitable. In fact, this intertwined issue of money and stepchildren can be the single most devastating obstacle you face in your marriage. Why? If you both have children, you might be able to use *your* child support (if you *get* some) to pay for their personal needs. Great. Or maybe you both agree that each pays for his or her own biological children's personal needs. But if you have one child, and he has three, how will that work? And what if he has three teenagers who want everything, and you have no biological children—that arrangement can put a huge drain on his monetary situation while leaving you free and clear. Also, the financial arrangement each of you has with the "ex" comes into play as well.

Here's where the majority of problems arise: If you set up a household budget and join even *part* of your money, income, and resources, and either his or your children put a drain on those funds that one of you does not perceive is healthy or fair, your issues about everything to do with kids and finances will be magnified. Set up a plan with an objective outside advisor who can help you determine the expenses you will face and suggest a plan for paying for them, then make an effort to stick to the program. Again, we can't give you the "right way" to arrange who pays for things the kids need—every situation is different. The secret is to find mutual agreement and make important decisions up front.

If one of you has the attitude that "These are my kids, I make the money, and I can give them what I choose," the union you strive to achieve won't happen. You may not care at first, but eventually you will, unless your husband or you have an unlimited financial reserve. Since that's not usually the case, pay close attention to this pivotal issue, which can make or break your chances of becoming another statistic.

Debts: His and Yours

Hopefully each of you has some resources that you are bringing into the relationship, even if it's only a few sticks of furniture. Oftentimes one or the other may also come with bills or outstanding debt as well. If he doesn't mind picking up the tab for yours, or the reverse, then great. Again, the key is deciding what is *fair* and working out a plan for each payment and/or responsibility. If you think you can do this alone, good luck, and go for it. But we found the emotion wrapped around money issues, especially debt, to be monumental—maybe not in the beginning when the "glow" is lingering, but eventually it can become a major source of conflict. But if you love your spouse *and* the kids enough, don't let the issue of debt ruin your chances for a happy existence. If you and your partner feel over your head in figuring out what you owe and who should pay for it, ask for help. Find a professional advisor to offer some suggestions.

Health Care

Decisions about who's paying for aspects of health care may have been made before you arrived on the scene of this relationship. Whatever your situation may be, compromising on health care is something neither of you should ever do. Decide which plan(s) affords you the best coverage. Whether you are all on one health insurance plan or separate ones, be sure to research what is most affordable for your family. For example, maybe it's equitable for all parties if his children (or yours) are on the other biological parent's plan and you pick up the difference in deductibles and any additional costs. If you are worried about the costs, ask the insurance company if they offer payment schedules.

Keeping your family physically and emotionally healthy is paramount. Don't skip emotional needs, whether it's on your health plan or not—this includes you, him, and the children. You're all facing life-altering changes and may need some help sorting through your feelings. Neglecting mental or emotional issues can be just as devastating as major physical conditions.

Other Insurance Issues

Yes, these affairs can get slightly complicated—sometimes to the point where they are so inconvenient that you avoid them altogether. We'll offer a few universal suggestions here, but keep in mind that all situations are unique. Here are the major insurance needs you'll likely have:

- Ample life insurance to carry your family through some tough years should certain unthinkable events occur
- Health insurance (discussed in the previous section)
- Disability coverage

Assuming you agree with the foregoing suggestions, here are ten issues to familiarize yourself with before having a talk with your insurance agent(s). A number of these have been touched upon in previous chapters:

1. Number and ages of children for whom you and/or your husband are responsible
2. Child support owed to and/or by ex-spouses
3. Children's current and future educational expenses
4. Your own age and health status as well as that of your husband and all children
5. Basic living costs going forward, including food, housing, utilities, auto, taxes, insurance, vacations, entertainment, and more
6. Total assets, obligations, and current incomes of both you and your husband
7. Who are to be the beneficiaries? What are their needs and lifestyles?
8. Outstanding debts, mortgages, and adverse judgments
9. Existing life, health, and disability coverage
10. Anticipated responsibilities and costs of other family members

Do not procrastinate in getting life and disability insurance. Even though no one wants to think about a time when you might need to use these investments, it is best to be prepared. One unanticipated hospital stay could render you hundreds of thousands of dollars in debt.

What type of insurance should you get? That depends on your specific needs. Companies differ widely in quality and quantity of coverage. Do your research and comparisons. If you're not aware of the specifics of your current coverage on various life and health issues, find out now. Ask your insurance agent for an item-by-item review of your policies, then decide if anything needs to change.

Believe it or not, financial losses can sometimes be greater if a person becomes disabled than if he dies. None of us wants to be an expensive burden. Check if you have that type of protection and the amounts thereof. It is wonderfully comforting to know that your incomes will continue indefinitely should disability occur either to you or your husband.

Retirement Accounts

Think you're too young to even think about retirement? Don't believe it for a minute. Retirement will come—don't let it come before you've planned for it. IRAs, Roth IRAs, Keogh plans, company-matched retirement and savings plans—each has unique features that could comprise a book all its own. You and your partner will likely find that a growing savings reserve is both confidence building and a satisfying accomplishment.

Some of you may be thinking that you have too many other expenses and debts to pay off before you can think about saving for retirement. And your current expenses may be high, yes. But many folks overspend their incomes on items they don't really need that depreciate rapidly after being purchased (such as expensive cars or multimedia equipment). When considering these big-ticket items, ask yourselves whether you can instead live with something that's a little less expensive and put the "savings" into your retirement account.

Consider an IRA

Roth IRAs are a favorite vehicle for building a retirement account. All dividends and interests earned are nontaxable. Savings build and compound, making them a terrific tool! Standard IRAs and other such plans build as well and are tax-deferred until you withdraw from them at retirement age.

If you don't know what plans you're currently enrolled in, meet with a financial advisor or your company's Human Resources representative and ask questions. Many companies will match your chosen savings amount to a certain level. Think about it: If your company should match fifty cents on the dollar, for every $100 you put into that account each month, the company will immediately give you $50 more! And the entire amount is invested to earn interest and/or purchase stock. How can you afford *not* to be involved to the maximum allowable level? (You may be able to withdraw from these accounts early if you need cash, but often with high penalties.)

The Kids' Post–High School and College Expenses

Many parents say, "I want my kids to have a better education than I had." That's a very good thing. However, it does cost money—usually a lot of money.

It's possible that these financial responsibilities were worked out in the divorce agreement, but some states do not allow stipulations in divorce decrees specifying to what

degree each parent is responsible for post–high school educational costs. (Many states only stipulate monetary support
until age eighteen.) In such states, you get to negotiate all
over again about the educational issues.

How Much Are We Talking About?

Just how much does it cost? Vocational technical schools
report a yearly tuition of $5,000 for what is considered a typical
"full load" of courses depending on the curriculum taken. State
universities typically charge yearly tuition costs ranging from
$8,000 to $10,000. Ivy league universities' (the Harvards, Princ-
etons, and Yales) yearly tuition alone may run from $35,000
to $50,000 depending on whether one is an undergraduate, a
graduate student, or in a professional school such as medicine
or law school. Bear in mind that your student hasn't eaten yet.
Nor does he have a place to live, clothing, books, or car. You
can fill in the rest. You could easily be faced with a $50,000 to
$300,000 bill to send just one of your children to college.

How Will We Ever Pay for That?

Breathe, breathe. Paying for college is daunting, but not
impossible. Start by gathering information, then research-
ing your options. Involve, of course, the child going to college, but also other children who may benefit from getting a
glimpse into what's in their future.

The first questions to ask are:

1. What school is best for your child's interests and abilities? If the teen is undecided, it may be best to begin
   with a general course of study and become informed in
   progress about whether he or she likes the school or not,
   as well as the selection of a major.

2. What are the total costs including tuition, food, housing, books, travel, and other expenses at the school(s) of choice?
3. Will your student work? If so, how much can be realistically earned?
4. Will a full or partial load be taken? How much time in years will the course of study take? What about scholarships and student loans?

Collegiate admission counselors can be of great help to the family in addressing these specific questions.

Once you have the answers to those questions, you can begin figuring out how much you have saved already and how much you'll need to borrow. For post–high school and collegiate expenses, there are a number of financial vehicles that can be very helpful. These include 529 plans and other such state-approved plans, which can be started virtually at the time of the child's birth. Monies deposited in them will compound and grow totally tax-free, provided all amounts are used for specific and legitimate educational expenses. Many such state plans allow income tax deductions to a certain level as well, amounting to further savings. Ask your financial advisor about these plans.

Students who work for a portion of their expenses can help. Scholarships can be a boon as well. And yes, student loans can defray costs. But please beware here: many graduate school students end up amassing loans and accrued interest of $100,000 to $200,000—staggering sums to repay upon graduation.

His and Your Child Support and Alimony Payments

Child support and alimony can add up to big money. Courts typically estimate the specific figures to be paid based on the income and assets of each parent and the children's needs.

Are they always fair? Certainly not. But they are what they are.

Negotiating Payments for the First Time

If you're reading this before divorce settlements have been finalized, try to use foresight to anticipate changes down the road. Costs of living rarely decrease, so if possible, have clauses inserted into the settlement agreement regarding necessary adjustments for cost of living increases.

Changing Current Payments

If your partner's (or your) settlement has already been reached, are you out of luck? No, payments can be changed in the event of unanticipated increases or decreases in income levels. But be prepared for costly legal expenses with no guarantees. Your case will need to be strong.

Take the example of former stepmom Becky, who filed suit to have her child support for her daughter increased by nearly 80 percent. Becky reasoned that during the eight years since her divorce settlement, costs of living had increased significantly. Her husband's income remained at a high level. When questioned privately by the judge, Becky's daughter Kelly waffled somewhat about her custody preference. Weighing that indecision as well as other issues, the judge decided to order joint rather than primary custody, as it had been, and cut child support payments to Becky in half. A devastating decision—and quite the reverse of what she hoped for.

Not all cases are as dramatic as this, but our point is made. Early decisions are often hard to change. Be aware as well that your new husband may be called into court by his ex-wife seeking increases of some sort. And sometimes, ex-wives do win.

Full Disclosure

Regardless of whether a settlement is final or not, do you know all of your family's financial obligations? If not, find out how much of the family income is received or must go to child support and/or alimony. Be sure you tell him your side as well: if you do not have custody, you may owe certain sums for child support. Your husband should know about all your obligations and receipts prior to any legal agreements.

Accountants inform us that child support payments are not tax deductible, whereas alimony payments are.

Family Obligations

Besides the usual bills and insurance fees, your family may have special circumstances involving someone's need to help a family member in financial ways. Here are two of the most common situations that arise.

Aging Parents

Unfortunately, health rarely gets better with age. That said, people today have better health habits than ever before, and they're paying dividends in many ways. Insurance agents tell us that people are increasingly living longer—you've no doubt heard of people in their nineties living by themselves who still drive and are self-sufficient.

That scenario, of course, is not always the case. Either you or your husband, or both, may feel an obligation to one or more of your aging parents to the extent that you may choose to provide housing, food, and care for them due to their failing health or lack of financial resources. Obviously, this can have a major impact depending upon the degree of care needed. One of you may have to alter your work schedule or stop working altogether. Your own family income and housing space may thus be compromised. Your family may lose privacy. The kids may feel resentment about space and privacy losses as well as other changes.

If you've maintained open and honest communication with your partner, you probably know about these situations or one that's on the horizon. It is one thing to know and be able to anticipate and plan. It is another to have to alter your best-laid plans for the future. Knowing in advance allows you to lay the groundwork in terms of selecting ample housing, financial planning, work scheduling, and informing and emotionally preparing the children.

Don't look at this as a burden. The process can be a satisfying and even rewarding venture for the entire family. The kids may come to enjoy helping out and spending time with grandparents. They may also come to appreciate having another caring adult at hand who has the wisdom of years.

Other Family Members

It's not always a parent who might require care from you or your husband. Other relatives, including grandparents, siblings, aunts, uncles, or even a close friend needing help may show up at your door. Any one of these individuals may have physical or emotional health issues. Life may not have been kind to them financially in spite of, or because of, their habits. Perhaps you or your husband may at one time have made a promise to help one of them.

Almost all of the impacting issues discussed in relation to aging parents apply to caring for other family members as well. The important issue, again, is that both marital partners should know the details of the other's obligations and promises in advance. Knowing allows one's partner to come to respect his/her mate for their humanity. It also allows you to make necessary preparations together.

A Case in Point: Compromise Is the Magic Word

Elizabeth brought two daughters of her own into a new marriage with Darien and his two girls. Elizabeth was well meaning but was used to giving her daughters just about everything they asked for. Darien was more conservative and made his teens work for the money he gave them. His older daughter even worked after school and was responsible for purchasing many of her own clothes and school-related things.

The household soon became rather unbalanced with two girls who didn't expect handouts and two who did. Elizabeth didn't think her girls' lifestyles should have to change just because Darien was so frugal. But before long, Elizabeth had major credit card expenses to add to the debt she was already carrying. Resentment and conflict started taking over the relationship. Before total disaster struck, they sought marriage counseling. "I had no idea something like this would become such an issue," Elizabeth told us. "In my first marriage, my husband never objected to any money that I spent on the girls. This was a huge adjustment."

Darien and Elizabeth's counselor helped them create a family budget and assigned specific responsibilities to each, and also to the girls.

REFLECTIONS: KEY ISSUES IN CHAPTER 13

- Many unanticipated money issues arise during remarriage.

- How you insist on spending money says so much about your character and adaptability.

- Whether it's about household or auto expenses, the kids' expenses, handling debts, health care, or insurance costs, the underlying necessity is a mutually agreed–upon plan and adherence to same.

- Start immediately in planning for retirement.

- Educational and college costs include issues such as the particular school or college chosen, length of study, scholarships, student loans, whether students will work, and their ultimate employability.

- How the paying or receipt of child support is handled is yet another issue to address.

- Find out if either of you has potential responsibilities to certain family members that might affect the new family.

Chapter 14

When to Call 911

When do things get beyond your control and skills? At what point do you need special professional intervention, advice, and an objective ear? Sometimes, this point is less than clear. You might hear, "Boys will be boys," or, "She's just going through a phase—she'll grow out of it," from well-meaning friends and relatives. It's easy to believe these theories—particularly when it's convenient for you.

Medical Situations

Most medical emergencies are quite apparent; we're not going to literally tell you when to call 911. However, you may easily overlook or minimize certain other situations in the chaos of merging your families. Some may progress to more serious consequences, when they may have yielded to, or benefited from, early treatment. Consider conditions such as adolescent-onset diabetes, allergies, asthma, obesity, pneumonia, pediatric HIV, adolescent rheumatoid arthritis, meningitis, blood disorders, malignancies, seizure disorders, vision and dental disorders, substance abuse and addictions (covered later in this chapter), ADD and ADHD, certain viral and bacterial infections, and sexually transmitted diseases. That's quite a list.

At any rate, do not allow such symptoms as fatigue, listlessness, breathing difficulties, coughing, weight changes, or others to linger before seeing your pediatrician or family doctor. Be sure everyone in the household gets regular medical checkups.

Legal Issues

Legal issues? Oh yes, as in:

- Whose insurance covers the kids—yours or the ex-spouse's?
- Might one parent have changed jobs or been terminated and forgot to tell you that his or her insurance changed? Maybe he or she is just temporarily unemployed and thought temporary coverage wasn't necessary? You mean the kids aren't covered right now and little Matt just had an appendectomy?
- Has coverage changed dramatically? Imagine that you thought fourteen-year-old Jacob, who just knocked out his two front teeth, had great dental insurance—but then you find out it only covered regular checkups.
- Can his or your ex really sue you for not getting a child to the doctor sooner?

These are just a few of the stories reported by stepmoms. Honestly, we're not trying to scare you. We're trying to make sure you are as prepared as possible. Skyrocketing medical/dental costs can dig deep financial pits. As we covered in Chapter 13, see that there is ample coverage on everyone your family is responsible for at all times—particularly when divorces and job changes occur. It's the eleventh hour here. Do you know where the policies are? Do not totally trust an ex-spouse's insurance coverage on your precious children. If you are unsure as to details, call the agent in question. Knowledge is powerfully protective and reassuring. If you feel at all unsure, ask a professional. This is not a time to assume or guess.

Sometimes, the villain might be the insurance policy itself. Policies are written by legal experts, usually much in their company's favor. If in doubt, have policies studied by a trusted expert or your own attorney so you're aware of some of the common snags:

- Waiting periods before coverage actually begins
- Limitations on how much coverage will be provided
- Restrictions as to preexisting conditions

In summary, there are innumerable situations where legal disputes must be settled in court. Need we tell you that legal costs are expensive—even when you win? Still, lawyers can serve as powerful friends and allies.

Ongoing Unresolved Conflicts

You, your partner, or one of your children may need outside intervention for continued conflicts between family members that may have intensified over time. This can happen with any child or adult.

Teens

You may find that you and your partner need help resolving conflicts that are inevitable during this period of a child's emotional development. After all, he is adapting to a new family life while dealing with his own changing body and mind. One scenario you may encounter is when the teen wants increasing privileges and you and your husband resist. Don't assume this is a phase or that it will work itself out—get help from a trained professional who knows how to deal with such situations.

Frustrations with Changes in Life?

Any of you might be struggling with ongoing resentments for unwanted life changes. These can be accelerated by ex-spouses and/or the most trivial of adult statements or behaviors. Often, kids' aggression is displaced, but rooted in these resentments. That is, the anger is really felt toward one person, but is projected on someone else. That someone else, unfortunately, may be you.

On some occasions, these feelings can reach a point of verbal or physical assault, as we address in the next section. Equally uncomfortable can be a state of tension between an adult and child or between any of the children. Here are some tips to deal with this situation:

- Sometimes, parents can be the mediators, using conflict resolution steps as outlined in Chapter 3.
- Show the power of forgiveness and its ability to defuse differences.
- Ask school counselors to help.
- Should these and other interventions not improve harmony, it is time for outside professional intervention. Your friends, the school, or your family doctor can recommend effective mental health experts with family counseling skills. The selected therapist may request that other family members be seen as well. This is good practice, as the entire family is more than likely in disharmony. It's like

an intricate hanging mobile. Pull on one unit and all others get in disarray.

Generally, insurance bears the majority of expense of mental health counseling. Please check this out in advance, or you might create financial problems.

Physical and Verbal Aggression in the Family

If the above-mentioned conflict manifests into physical and/or verbal aggression, it becomes an extremely volatile and threatening situation. At no time should any physical aggression be tolerated; it requires immediate intervention. Never, ever should a child be allowed to show physical aggression toward any other person in the family, but in particular, a parent. Nor should you or your partner use any kind of physical discipline on a child.

We are aware that siblings and stepsiblings get into spats and shouting matches, and that is part of growing up and family life. You should be able to identify when it moves beyond minor squabbles and becomes more serious. Intervene at such a time and evaluate the situation. You as a parent have the responsibility to model appropriate and respectful behavior. We recognize that kids can make us all a little crazy at any age, and maybe that is part of their job. But responding with verbal or physical aggression is not an option. You don't get to lose it, because being the adult is part of your job.

Equally as harmful and dangerous, if not more so, is verbal abuse and aggression. It is the silent killer of a person's self-esteem and self-worth. It is obviously not as overtly visible as physical abuse, but its damage can be deep and far-reaching. Again, it's your responsibility to demonstrate respectful dialogue and interaction. Everyone loses his temper and yells now and then. If you do, apologize. Act like the adult and avoid verbal arguments and power struggles. It's not worth it. As with all things, choose your battles.

You should not tolerate disrespectful language or conduct toward you, your spouse, or the other children in the family. If you cannot deal with it alone, now is the time to seek help from a medical professional and/or counselor. Don't hesitate to face it immediately when it starts; if left unchecked, it will only escalate.

Substance Abuse and Addictions

Let us count the ways. Consider alcohol and marijuana—the two most widely abused drugs by children, adolescents, and adults. But the list goes on: sniffing of glue and propellants; party and date rape drugs like ecstasy, Rohypnol, GHA, and Ketamine (which are especially dangerous in that they are tasteless, odor free, and easily added to drinks so their victims are unable to make sound decisions and are often rendered unconscious and easy prey); speed drugs like methamphetamines, cocaine, and crack; and the highly addictive opiates, including heroin, morphine, and many synthetic narcotics like Percodan, Vicodin, Demerol, and Darvon.

An extensive list, to say the least. Unfortunately, you may find a family member turning to one of these substances to deal with the changes and/or problems that he or she feels that the blended family has created. Make sure you research and understand each major category for specific effects.

Marijuana

The dangers of most of the "hard-core" drugs are obvious. But let's discuss marijuana and its deceptions. Kids, and even some adults, often say, "Pot is just recreational. It's harmless and not involved in accidents like alcohol. It should be legalized." Don't believe it. Here is why: The greatest overall harm from smoking marijuana is the destruction of motivation. Kids might have the best intentions of getting that term paper done or finishing a list of tasks. Then they take one hit of marijuana. Result? Term paper and tasks are put on hold. The fact is, they may never get done.

Pot smoke is more carcinogenic than tobacco smoke, puff for puff. It can result in neurological damage, memory loss, and birth defects. Adults, while smoking, are not emotionally available to their children. Like all the above drugs, marijuana is addictive and expensive.

Be Proactive and Prevent

Preventing teenage drug abuse is a better idea than trying to stop it once it's started. How do you prevent it? By being there for your child, encouraging healthy activities and involvements, practicing active listening, and being a mature model. Don't review your own adolescent mistakes at this time. Being that totally interested and encouraging parent, with whom it is easy to talk, as well as being an excellent role model, makes it much more difficult for them to disappoint you.

How Do I Know If a Child Is on Drugs?

What are the symptoms if you suspect your kids may be currently using? Here are some big ones: drop in grades, loss of interest in school and related activities, different friends, changes in temperament and outlook, ignored responsibilities, drug stashes and paraphernalia, poor nutrition, health deterioration, money missing from purses, and drug selling. Use your favorite search engine to find one of the many excellent online parent quizzes regarding additional clues to teenage drug use.

What Do I Do If My Child Is Using Drugs?

Be especially vigilant regarding his or her whereabouts, activities, and friends. Confront the child in a firm but accepting manner. If it's your partner's child and he's around, he should lead the discussion—but don't wait for him to return if something happens and you're the only one home. Have the child download information about the drugs in question. Then seek a certified drug and alcohol counselor in your area and get the child into treatment. Remove privileges and install a finite grounding period. The child can become ungrounded and regain privileges by getting involved in treatment. You and your partner should become involved in the treatment as requested. Drug and alcohol counselors will likely request a family history, as proneness to abuse and addictions is highly genetic.

Academic Problems and School Behavior

Every parent dreads the unsolicited contact from the child's teacher or school principal indicating that a problem exists. As we have addressed in previous chapters, you have a responsibility to be supportive of your child's academic needs, behavior, and school performance. Children undergoing such a life change as a parent's remarriage are likely to encounter at least a brief period of academic struggle.

Academic Deficiencies

Work in tandem with the school, in particular your child's teacher, to determine academic levels, needs, problems or issues, and what you can do at home to support that. If academic problems become more than you can handle, seek help from the school's counselor or student support group. He or she can generally advise you as to a course of action. The child may need a psychological evaluation to identify a learning disability or other special need. The school can usually advise you with regard to outside tutoring or academic resources.

Don't turn a blind eye thinking it's the school's problem alone to educate your child. You have to show your child you are willing to assist in any way you can and work together in a cooperative partnership. Granted, you are not the teacher, but success for your child's future is largely determined by how interested and invested in his or her achievements you appear. It takes time, effort, and a lot of work to assist a child with academic problems. It's all part of the package, however, and your efforts will show your child how much you care about him or her and what he or she can achieve.

Bad Behavior

Behavior problems are something that teachers wish they never had to address. Telling a parent his or her child has behavior issues is not an easy thing to do, but it's the teacher's responsibility to do so. As unpleasant as it is for school personnel (and it is unpleasant), it is probably even harder for you to hear. You may be told that your child or stepchild is disruptive, aggressive toward others, disrespectful, or displaying some other undesirable behaviors. It could be a passive–aggressive form of academic involvement, like refusing to do school work or hand in assignments.

THINK OF THE CHILD'S CLASSMATES

Whatever the behavioral problem may be, it is your responsibility to work out a plan with the school for changing it. As with members of your family, there should be zero tolerance for physical or verbal aggression. Nor can you tolerate a child who disrupts the learning of others by acting out. Parents who ignore school reports of disruptive behavior often do not take into account how their child may be adversely affecting the learning of every other child in the classroom. Not only does it interrupt instruction, but it takes the teacher's time when he or she has to respond to it.

INCLUDE THE CHILD

Include the child in question when developing a behavior plan with the school that includes consequences as well as rewards. Once it's finalized, do your part and stick to it. We do not advocate rewarding children for behavior that should be expected, but we are aware that it's difficult for some to make changes, and rewards can help reach a positive outcome.

Seeing that you and your spouse address the problem together is a way to make sure the child doesn't pit you against each other. Kids with behavior issues can be quite manipulative in figuring out how to get out of trouble with a poor school report. Be vigilant—listen to both sides, and be realistic with your goals and expectations. Things take time, but change can be achieved if you truly care about your child's or stepchild's future.

Okay—now, along with all of this advice, we're throwing you another challenge. You also have to be your child's advocate and make sure the school's concerns about behavior are legitimate. Don't just naturally assume the child is guilty or completely at fault. Investigate the situation as best you can and, again, work in tandem with the school. You both have the same goals for the child.

Conduct Disorders Including Theft, Assault, and Property Damage

Theft, assault, and property damage are serious aberrations of behavior that incur legal consequences. If your child or stepchild commits any of these felonies, the courts will likely require counseling for the child or adolescent involved as well as his/her parents.

What are the aggravating factors behind these acts? Most often, considerable anger is involved. The assailant may have been a victim of some type of abuse or neglect. Antisocial acts may be the result of an incubation of this anger over time. Parents might have been a huge source of disappointment. As a result, there can even be a sense of entitlement for what a child has gone through. Or, sadly, the child may simply be modeling an adult who actively engages in such behavior.

Parents and counselors can bring an adolescent to realize that Mom or Dad may not have had the opportunity to learn to parent well. The child might come to empathize with a parent who may have had a difficult home life as well. A degree of forgiveness and acceptance may follow. Many children perceive that "other kids have it so much better," when such may actually not be the case. When kids see life's imperfections as a challenge rather than a threat, attitudes can change and good things can happen. Kids can learn to visualize positive purposes that can steer them in constructive directions. Set useful goals fashioned to his or her abilities to help this developing person abandon bad behaviors for good.

A Case in Point: Unhealthy Influence

Rachel's stepson, Brad, age fourteen, had been in minor trouble with his "friends" from school and the neighborhood. She and her husband were convinced he was hanging out with the wrong crowd but were hesitant to limit his contact completely, knowing that would make the group even more appealing. But when the boys pushed the envelope too far by spray-painting the car of a minority family in the neighborhood, they knew a more intense response was necessary. They turned him in to the police, where he was arrested for vandalism and a hate crime.

Even though he was released to them, he was put on probation and forced to make restitution and do community service. "It was the hardest thing we ever did," said Rachel. "We knew this was a cry for help on his part, but we couldn't handle it alone." Brad is now in counseling and knows he has to be accountable for his actions. He is aware that his parents love and support him, but will never tolerate breaking the law or disrespecting the rights and property of others without a serious consequence.

REFLECTIONS: KEY ISSUES IN CHAPTER 14

- Major health emergencies are usually obvious. Become attuned to the more subtle symptoms, which may signal significant health concerns.

- Avoid unwelcome surprises. See that the children, you, and your husband are well covered for all medical and dental situations.

- Continuing or worsening family conflicts signal the need for outside professional intervention.

- Do not tolerate physical and verbal aggressions. Separate the combatants. Use conflict resolution procedures. If necessary, enlist help from outside mental health and juvenile justice personnel.

- Be aware of the signs of substance abuse and addictions. Seek addiction counselors if necessary.

- Work in cooperation with school specialists regarding academic and school behavior problems. Seek special tutors and professional counseling if necessary.

- Severe conduct issues such as theft, assault, and property damage usually bring perpetrators in contact with the law. Often the courts will mandate special psychiatric treatment. If not, make it your business to seek it out.

Chapter 15

Job Satisfaction for the Effective Stepmom

Okay, after fourteen chapters that outline one menacing minefield after another, what's the good news? Can dealing with his kids bring blessings? Are there really some potential feel-good stories in store? The answer is a resounding yes—though they may not happen at the time or in the manner you expect or hope them to. All that matters, of course, is that they do happen, because can you really put a price on positively impacting children's lives and their future families and communities? The stepmoms we interviewed shared many heartwarming and encouraging scenarios.

What job is more important—and, yes, challenging—than that of a parent or stepparent? What makes it important and challenging is also what makes it so rewarding and fulfilling. Nothing easy, after all, brings about a truly fulfilling sense of satisfaction. Think of the grueling training morning to night, day after day, endured by Olympic athletes. Now, think of the euphoric thrill of winning a medal or simply being an Olympic participant. As a stepmom, you are dealing with influencing other human beings (and their offspring) for the rest of their lives. It is the toughest job you will ever love. Learn how you can get much more than you give.

Easily the Most Important Job in the World

Note that we didn't say it's the easiest job in the world—just one of the most important. No matter how much joy you derive from being a parent, it's also a job. Being a stepmom requires a special kind of person; you have to face so many constantly changing variables that are out of your control. Loving the children may be the easy part. Finding your place in their lives, hearts, and future is the challenge.

Divorce is difficult for children of any age. Many disruptions take place, and confusions occur that the kids didn't deserve or ask for. You can make the difference between chaos and stability, failure and success, and happiness and misery. You don't have to get up each morning asking yourself, "What wonderful things can I do for them today?" What you can do is wake up thinking that you will be the best mom or stepmom possible. You have the power to play a role in determining what kind of people these children will be. You can't control another person's behavior, but you can help mold and shape it by your own.

Yes, It's Challenging,
but It's Also Immensely Rewarding

You might not think there are many (if any) rewards when you're picking up dirty clothes, scrubbing dishes, listening to whining about homework, and transporting kids to various obligations and destinations. Keep telling yourself that these days are numbered, and what you do now builds lives for the future and determines where you will all find yourselves at the end of the day. It might happen that some days you will be bored to death watching another soccer game and thinking about everything else you have to do. But one day, we hope you hear "Thanks for always being there for me. It meant a lot that you went to all of my school and sporting events."

When they walk across the stage at high school or college graduation, you will know that you had a part in forming their success.

You Can't Help Being a Model

For better or worse, studies universally suggest that children often choose role models who are prestigious, clever, talented, or attractive. Note kids' renewed interest in golf when Tiger Woods began winning his many golf tournaments. In the wake of Michael Phelps bringing home a record eight gold medals at the 2008 Beijing Olympic Games, interest in swimming instantly spiked.

Other nationally known people model wonderfully positive qualities of giving back to their communities and providing for those less fortunate than themselves. Others model less than positive images, particularly in their private lives. Perhaps they are oblivious to the fact that these negative antics impact children and youth everywhere who are in awe of their talents.

Of course, you can't control your children's famous role models, but you can control your own behavior. Kids tend to walk, talk, and think like their parents and/or significant others. Most are likely to adopt the same religion, politics, and philosophies as their parents, stepparents, or others they admire.

Are there exceptions to those patterns? Yes. A few kids think and behave in a manner directly opposite to their parents or stepparents. Such kids may do so because they perceive themselves to have been short-changed somehow. Others may view parents as being hypocritical, in that they might voice one set of ideals but behave otherwise.

Some positive examples of acting in an opposite manner occur when a parent, stepparent, or parent's significant other engages in significantly negative activities. Such behaviors may include substance use and addictions, self-defeating personality traits, and criminal behaviors. Children witnessing the devastating results of such acts may then decide never to use nonprescribed substances, engage in illegal acts, or display negative or phony character traits. Unfortunately, however, many kids *do* model the negative acts of their parents and stepparents.

What is the lesson here? It is that we cannot help being a model, either in positive or negative ways. Now that you know that you leave an indelible impression on kids, strive to use your powers for good. Do it for the kids and their future offspring. You want them to be the best they can be. They are your link to the future. Your influence can affect:

- Improved school performance
- Improved, even exemplary, behavior
- Higher vocational/professional aspirations
- Good citizenry

A supportive and stable home can greatly affect the future of the next generation. Do people pull themselves up from the dregs and make it on their own? Yes. Do people from good, loving, and supportive homes fall flat? Yes. But, statistically, kids coming from a home that fosters high ideals, values, and goals, have a better chance to become successful, productive, and contributing members of society.

It's the Toughest Job You'll Ever Love

Yesteryear's Peace Corps slogan, "It's the toughest job you'll ever love," was both appealing and authentic. Peace Corps work was tough. It meant working long, hard days physically and emotionally, doing whatever that particular community needed, be it building structures, or ministering to the sick. But volunteers reaped enormous satisfaction from seeing the results of their labors and the appreciation from those who were helped.

Further testimonials regarding the rewards of putting oneself on the line for others come from the many adult mission groups associated with churches and other agencies throughout the country who travel around the world to give of themselves. It may be a surgeon correcting cleft palates, or a worker who helps build a home or church. The universal report of the workers is, "I brought back so much more than I took." Each experiences and embraces the total joy of giving of themselves for the right reasons.

Being a stepmom is tough at times, too. Wise stepmoms anticipate and plan for the tough times, but they also live the slogan, "When the going gets tough, the tough get going." You labor, learn, and experiment for their benefit and yours. Life without learning is standing still. Watch for the baby-step improvements of those for whom you are responsible. Reward and rejoice when you see signs of positive growth. Sometimes there are temporary setbacks. Growth is never an exclusively upward endeavor. It fluctuates, but, most importantly, the overall direction is up. Yes, it can be tough. But it is a labor of love.

Giving Is Getting

Giving of ourselves for the betterment of someone in need (like your husband's kids) is a very good thing. Giving out of a sense of guilt, with the goal of gaining recognition or making the recipient feel obligated, or in a way that results in a learning experience being lost or in degradation or harm are all based on negative motivations—not the type that kids should witness.

Giving is getting? Yes. It's quite okay to privately experience the joy of giving and to observe a recipient's relief and appreciation. Seeing a child turn in a positive direction is an unequaled satisfaction. Giving provides powerfully positive lessons for kids. They will likely come to embrace generosity as well.

Go for It

You are now armed with suggestions, techniques, and examples regarding building relationships with stepkids, dealing with special children, custody arrangements, cooperating with the biological mom, sharing Daddy, creating your own family rituals, discipline, and more. Perhaps all this might have made you a bit cautious about becoming a stepmom. That's mostly a good thing. Such a mindset enables you to be less starry-eyed and much more realistic in your thinking and expectations. You know that time and patience is necessary.

It should be comforting for you to know that many veteran stepmoms interviewed regarded their experience as both broadening and enriching. Many reported that their stepkids now have their own families but still voluntarily stay in contact with them. Many such stepkids now understand the effort, the parents being there for them and hanging in there when things were tough, and the continued caring they received. The moms most appreciated were the ones who showed them the right way; taught them by example; and had clear expectations, rewards, and consequences. These stepmoms were both compassionate and firm and always had the kids' best interests at heart.

You will make mistakes. Mistakes result in learning. No one learns very much when things go totally smoothly. Obstacles promote thinking and problem solving. Do basketball stars make every shot? No, but each miss teaches them what adjustments need to be made. Do not worry about making mistakes. Strive to learn. View being a stepmom as a challenge, not a threat.

A Case in Point: The Benefits Keep Going!

Cathy always handled most "people things" about as well as could be done. (She ranks right at the top of our list of great stepmoms.) Having a ten-year-old son from a previous relationship, she married a man with two daughters, thirteen and sixteen years of age. Two years later, she and her new husband had a son.

Her secrets? Cathy anticipated—and taught her family to anticipate—situations before problems developed. She was realistic. She had read, studied, and listened to experienced stepmoms. Most importantly, she made no distinction between his kids, her son, and the child they had together. Each child was unique and equally precious. Each was listened to and felt special. The kids sensed her fairness. They all quickly came to respect Cathy. Each child was a personal love project. As needed, Cathy was able to discipline and teach respect for family rules. One would expect that a husband of Cathy's would be involved, strong, and supportive, and he was. The family van rarely cooled. The children's interests were always attended by one or both parents

Did problems occur? Of course. Cathy took the attitude that, "Well, they told me this kind of stuff would happen." To her these were challenges, not threats.

Fifteen years after the marriage, Cathy, the mom, stepmom, and now grandstepmom reported, "I love it when they are all here. Each one brings something special to the table. Nothing feels better than the appreciation I get from them now." Indeed, the benefits go on and on for this happy stepmom.

REFLECTIONS: KEY ISSUES IN CHAPTER 15

- Can you think of a more challenging, important, and rewarding job than parenting?

- You have the duty and power to help and shape his kids and yours.

- We are all models all of the time, for better or for worse.

- Giving, if done humbly, cheerfully, and not to get anything in return, reaps great blessings.

- You are prepared now. Go for it. May you all reap those rewards.

Bibliography and Resources

Bibliography

Burns, Cherie. *Stepmotherhood: How to Survive Without Feeling Frustrated, Left Out, or Wicked.* New York: Three Rivers Press, 2001.

Deyo, Yaacov, and Deyo, Sue. *SpeedDating.* New York: HarperCollins Publishers, Inc., 2002.

Ellis, Albert. *A Guide to Rational Living.* Upper Saddle River, NJ: Prentice-Hall Inc., 2004.

Frankl, Viktor E. *Man's Search for Meaning.* Boston: Beacon Press, 2006.

Godek, Gregory J. P. *1001 Ways to Be Romantic.* Naperville, IL: Sourcebooks, Inc., 2007.

Howell, Patti, and Jones, Ralph. *World Class Marriage.* Montreal: HJ Books, 2002.

Ickes, William. *Empathic Accuracy.* New York: The Guilford Press, 1997.

Lutz, Erica. *The Complete Idiot's Guide to Stepparenting.* New York: Alpha Books, 1998.

Mack, Cassandra. *Young, Gifted and Doing It: 52 Power Moves for Teens.* New York: Strategies for Empowered Living, 2003.

McWilliams, P., Bloomfield, Harold H., and Colgrove, Melba. *How to Survive the Loss of a Love.* Los Angeles: Mary Books/Prelude Press, 2004.

Perry, Susan. *Loving in Flow: How the Happiest Act and Stay That Way.* Naperville, IL: Sourcebooks, Inc., 2003.

Ricci, Isolina. *Mom's House, Dad's House*. New York: Simon & Shuster, 1997.

Schwartz, Gary E. *The Afterlife Experiments*. New York: Atria Books, 2002.

Scuka, Robert. *Relationship Enhancement Therapy: Healing Through Deep Empathy and Intimate Dialogue*. New York: Routledge, 2005.

Visher, Emily B., and Visher, John S. *How to Win as a Stepfamily*. New York: Brunner-Routledge, 1991.

Winter, Judy. *Breakthrough Parenting for Children with Special Needs: Raising the Bar of Expectations*. San Francisco: Jossey-Bass, 2006.

Resources

American Association for Marriage and Family Therapy (AAMFT)
    1212 South Alfred Street
    Alexandria, VA 22314
    703-838-9808
    www.aamft.org

Association for Family and Conciliation Courts (AFCC)
    6525 Grand Teton Plaza
    Madison, WI 53719
    608-664-3750
    www.afccnet.org

Divorce Prevention and Marriage Enhancement Program (PREP)
    PO Box 4793
    Greenwood Village, CO 80155
    800-366-0166
    www.prepinc.com

National Institute of Relationship Enhancement (NIRE)
440 East West Hwy, Suite 28
Bethesda, MD 20814
800-4-FAMILIES
301-986-1479
www.nire.org

Parenting @ iVillage
parenting.ivillage.com
Covers parenting issues large and small, with expert advice and community forums.

Positive Steps
www.positivesteps.net
The Positive Steps Program acts as a prevention plan for children and adolescents who are experiencing early behavior problems at home, at school, or in their free time. The program also acts as an intervention for juvenile first offenders.

Practical Application of Intimate Relationship Skills (PAIRS)
www.pairs.com
The PAIRS programs, developed by Lori H. Gordon, Ph.D., provide a comprehensive system to enhance self-knowledge and to develop the ability to sustain pleasurable intimate relationships. Gordon's approach integrates a wide range of theories and methods from psychology, education, and psychotherapy and presents them in an educational format. PAIRS acts to bridge therapy, marital enrichment, and marriage and family development.

The Stepfamily Association of America
650 J. Street, Suite 205
Lincoln, NE 68508
402-477-7837

800-735-0329

www.stepfam.org

The Stepfamily Association of America is an educational organization that holds support meetings in chapters all across the country.

The Stepfamily Foundation, Inc.
333 West End Avenue
New York, NY 10023
212-877-3244
www.stepfamily.org

Since 1975, The Stepfamily Foundation, Inc. has provided counseling seminars for professions and information to help create a successful step relationship.

Strategies for Empowered Living
Cassandra Mack, CEO
www.strategiesforempoweredliving.com

Strategies for Empowered Living Inc. is a social enterprise that offers educational workshops, motivational keynotes, consultation services, and products that focus on personal growth and empowerment.

World Class Marriage Workshop
1045 Passiflora Avenue
Leucadia, CA 92024
866-879-3960
760-436-3960
www.worldclassmarriage.com

Information and classes for couples.

Index

Active listening, 12–13, 32–33

ADD/ADHD, 162, 210

Adoption of a stepchild, 77–78

Adult children, 5

Affection, bestowing, 48–49

Age of children. *See also* Adult
children; Preteens; Teenagers;
Younger children

discipline and, 130

disparities between yours and
his, 181–82

first meeting and, 4–5

friends and, 120

handling differences in, 182

stepmother's age in relation
to, 182

Aggression, physical and verbal,
5, 213–14, 218. *See also* Assault

Alimony payments, 203–5

Alone time with the kids

father's, 107–8

stepmother's, 111

Angry children. *See* Resistant and
angry children

Assault, 219. *See also* Aggression,
physical and verbal

Attention Deficit Disorder. *See*
ADD/ADHD

Authority, establishing, 45–46

Automobiles

financial responsibility for, 196

servicing, 153–55

Bedtime, 125–26

Biological mothers, 86–104

animosity between ex-spouse
and, 92–93

change in attitude toward, 101–3

children's bond with, 83

commending, 89–90

communicating with, 92,
96–98

cooperation *vs.* competition
with, 95–96

deceased, 69, 82

discipline and, 132, 137

discussing with the children,
93–95

handling negativity toward,
88–89

how to approach, 87–93

keeping disagreements private,
91

obtaining data on kids from, 90

putting at ease, 88

reassurances about her role, 91

religious issues and, 185

remarriage of, 99–101

respecting input from, 89

of special needs children, 39

Birthdays, 173–74

*Breakthrough Parenting for Children
with Special Needs* (Winter), 39

Index

Cars. *See* Automobiles

Cases in point
    biological mothers, 101–3
    criminal behavior, 220
    custody arrangements, 83
    discipline, 145
    fathers, 111
    financial issues, 207
    holidays, 175–76
    housing issues, 71
    mealtime, 126–27
    meeting the kids, 21
    religious differences, 188–89
    resistant children, 40
    school issues, 161–62
    spousal unity, 59–60
    stepmothering rewards, 228

Child custody. *See* Custody arrangements

Child support, 203–5

Chores, 147–52
    delegating responsibility for, 148
    involving the kids in, 149–52
    paying kids to do, 152
    picking one's battles, 149
    skills learned via, 151

Christmas, 166–69, 175–76

College education costs, 54–55, 201–3

Communication
    between biological and stepmothers, 92, 96–98
    with children, 43–44, 46–47
    in groups, 98
    nonverbal, 97–98
    verbal, 97
    written, 98

Companionate love, 51

Compressed speech, 12

Conduct disorders, 219

Confidante, becoming, 19–20

Conflicts
    ongoing unresolved, 211–13
    tactics for resolution, 47–48

Cooking, 148. *See also* Mealtime

Criminal behavior, 219, 220

Cultural differences, 20, 178–81
    childrearing practices, 180
    food preferences, 179–80
    language, 179
    modes of dress, 180–81

Curfew, 123–24, 136, 161

Custody arrangements, 73–84, 88
    adoption, 77–78
    family unit and subunits in, 73–74
    full/sole, 75, 76
    housing issues and, 62
    joint, 75, 76–77
    long-distance, 79–80
    the maternal bond and, 83
    primary, 75
    split, 75, 77
    transportation and, 81
    types of, 75–77
    unanticipated and renegotiated, 82–83

Debts, 197–98

Disability insurance, 199–200

Discipline, 129–46

ambiguous areas in, 139–40

appropriate consequences in, 136–37

consistency in, 141–42

disagreements with partners over, 140–41

establishing rules, 130–32

fairness in, 138–39

ongoing maintenance of, 140–42

resistance to, 130

rewards in, 133–35

saying "no," 59–60

when one parent is away, 141

Divorce, impact on children, 23–24, 223

Down syndrome, 39–40

Education. See School

eHarmony.com, 178

Exercise, 35–36

Fairness, 47–48, 138–39

Fathers, 105–12

discipline and, 130

hobbies of, 110

job/career and, 108–9

relationship with entire family, 107

relationship with his children, 9, 105–6

relationship with stepchildren, 106, 111

stay-at-home, 193

time with friends, 109

trips with his children, 107–8

Financial issues, 52–55, 191–208

child support and alimony, 203–5

compromising on, 207

debts, 197–98

education expenses, 54–55, 201–3

employment decisions, 191–93

family obligations, 205–7

full disclosure in, 205

honesty in, 53–54

joint vs. separate accounts, 193–94

payment plans, 195–200

retirement, 200–201

socioeconomic background, 183–84

stress-reduction tips, 194–95

529 plans, 203

Flexibility, 117–18

Food. See Mealtime

Friends (children's)

parental disapproval of, 173

proximity to, 68

standards and rules for, 119–22

troublemaking, 220

on vacations, 175

Friends (spouse's), 109

Full/sole custody, 75, 76

Gifts

birthday, 173–74

Christmans/holiday, 168

at first meeting, 7, 21

Index

Goal setting, 55–56
Godek, Greg, 52
Good behavior, reinforcing, 29
Grandchildren
   meeting, 8
   partner's relationship with, 107
Grandparents
   getting along with, 17
   housing issues and, 70–71

Health care
   common medical problems,
      209–10
   financial responsibility for, 198
Health insurance, 198, 210–11
Hobbies (spouse's), 110
Holidays, 166–69. *See also*
   Vacations
   disputes over, 175–76
   input from the kids on, 169
   making a success of, 168
   preparations for, 167–68
   structuring, 96
Homework, 155–58
   fostering independence, 156–57
   help and self-help, 118–19
   success checklist, 157–58
   the "what have you tried?"
      method, 157
   working with the school, 158
House maintenance, 153
Housing issues, 62–72
   children's input on, 65–66
   decorating and rearranging,
      69–70

his *vs.* her home, 63–64
in-laws' approval, 70–71
making a home, 71
a new abode, 65
physical structure of house,
   66–67
proximity to conveniences, 68–69
rules and, 131
temporary quarters, 67

"I" messages, 144–45
Imprinting, 18
In-laws, 70–71. *See also*
   Grandparents
Input (biological mother's), 89
Input (children's)
   on curfew, 124
   on holiday plans, 169
   on housing, 65–66
   on school-related problems, 218
   on vacation plans, 175
Insurance, 198–200
   automobile, 154, 196
   disability, 199–200
   health, 198, 210–11
   life, 199–200
Interests (children's)
   nurturing, 13–16
   rewards of knowing, 40
   seeking out, 30–31
Internet, monitoring use of, 119,
   170
Intimacy, spousal, 50–51
IRAs, 201

Jobs/careers, 108–9, 191–93
Joint custody, 75, 76–77

Language differences, 179
Lawn and garden maintenance, 153
Legal issues, 59, 210–11
Life insurance, 199–200
Listening, active, 12–13, 32–33
Long-distance stepparenting, 79–80

Mack, Cassandra, 17
Marijuana use, 214–15
Mealtime
    cooking responsibilities, 148
    culture and food preferences, 179–80
    etiquette and expectations, 115–18, 126–27
Meeting the kids, 3–12
    open-mindedness and, 3–4
    planning ahead for, 21
    preparation for, 6
    recipe for success, 7–8
    timing of, 4–5
    understanding required for, 6–7
Metaphoric stories, 33–35
Mirroring technique, 12
Mom's House, Dad's House (Ricci), 126
Money. *See* Financial issues
Mothers. *See* Biological mothers

Negative thinking
    about biological mothers, 88–89

redirecting, 27–29
New Age spirituality, 187–88
Nonverbal communication, 97–98
Number of children, 5

Occult, belief in, 187–88
1001 Ways to Be Romantic (Godek), 52

Paranormal, belief in, 187–88
Parents, care of aging, 205–6
Past, learning about, 24
Patience, 45, 114–15, 117–18
Pets, 67, 68, 81
Phelps, Michael, 224
Police, calling, 220
Positive behavior, modeling, 17–19, 29–30
Preteens, 120
Primary custody, 75
Privacy needs, 50, 67, 144
Property damage, deliberate, 219

Reframing technique, 28
Reinforcement, positive, 29
Relationship-building, 9–20
    active listening in, 12–13, 32–33
    by backing off, 25–27
    becoming a confidante, 19–20
    cultural differences and, 20
    by nurturing interests and needs, 13–16
    role modeling and, 17–19
    their expectations in, 11–12
    your expectations in, 10–11

Index

Religious and spiritual
  differences, 184–89
  biological parents and, 185
  finding a common ground,
    188–89
  issues involved in, 184–85
  presenting values and beliefs,
    186
  understanding, 185–86
Resistant and angry children,
  23–36
  backing off from, 25–27
  discerning reason for
    behavior, 23–25
  exercise for, 35–36
  learning about their past, 24
  learning interests of, 30–31,
    40
  metaphoric stories for, 33–35
  modeling positive behavior
    for, 29–30
  redirecting negative
    thinking, 27–29
  self-disclosure to, 31–33
Retirement accounts, 200–201
Rewards, 133–35, 218
Ricci, Isolina, 126
Role models
  for all behaviors, 224–25
  for positive behavior, 17–19,
    29–30
  for successful relationships, 49
Role-playing, 37–38
Romance, 51–52
Routines, establishing, 114–15

Rules
  establishing, 130–32
  for socializing with friends, 121

Schedules, creating, 14–15
School, 216–18
  academic problems, 216–17
  attending functions, 158–59
  behavioral problems, 217–18
  changing, 68, 82
  education needs and
    expenses, 54
  post-high school education
    costs, 54–55, 201–3
  working effectively with,
    161–62
  working with on homework
    problems, 158
Self-disclosure, 31–33
Self-esteem, 13
Sexual issues
  attraction between
    stepsiblings, 181–82
  attraction toward stepparent,
    51, 182–83
  for teenagers, 142
Shy children, 36–38
  behavior demonstration for,
    36–37
  discerning reason for
    behavior, 23–25
  focusing outward and, 37
  role-playing for, 37–38
  social practice for, 38
Siblings and stepsiblings

adding another, 56–58

age differences in, 181–82

Sleepovers, 171–73

Social rewards, 134

Socioeconomic background, 183–84

Special needs children, 38–40

Split custody, 75, 77

Spouses, 42–61

    adjustment period and, 44–45

    bestowing affection, 48–49

    communication and, 43–44, 46–47

    conflict resolution, 47–48

    establishing authority, 45–46

    as first priority, 44

    having another child, 56–58

    intimacy needs, 50–51

    maintaining relationship strength, 50–52

    presenting a united front, 121, 149

    privacy needs, 50

    as relationship role models, 49

    romance between, 51–52

    as a single entity, 42–43

    teamwork in, 46–49

    time spent together, 110–11

Stay-at-home parents, 192–93

Stepfamily Association of America, 78

Strategies for Empowered Living Inc., 17

Substance abuse and addictions, 214–16

"Taxi" stepmoms, 81

Teamwork, 46–49

Teenagers

    cars and, 154–55

    chores and, 150–52

    conflicts with, 211–12

    discipline of, 142–45

    friends of, 120

    meeting, 5, 7

Theft, 219

Transportation, 81, 160–61

Vacations, 169–71. *See also* Holidays

    family, 174–75

    input from the kids on, 175

    planning ahead for, 170–71

    structuring, 96

Verbal communication, 97

Violence. *See* Aggression, physical and verbal; Assault; Criminal behavior

Visher, Emily B., 78

Visher, John S., 78

Visitation, 96. *See also* Custody arrangements

Warren, Neil Clark, 178

Wicca, 188

Winter, Judy, 39

Woods, Tiger, 224

Written communication, 98

"You" messages, 144–45

Younger children

    friends of, 120

    meeting, 5